MAX-PLANCK-GESELLSCHAFT

Universität
Augsburg
University

TECHNISCHE
UNIVERSITÄT
MÜNCHEN

THE GEORGE
WASHINGTON
UNIVERSITY

WASHINGTON, DC

**MIPLC Studies**
Edited by

Prof. Dr. Christoph Ann, LL.M. (Duke Univ.)
TUM School of Management

Prof. Robert Brauneis
The George Washington University Law School

Prof. Dr. Josef Drexl, LL.M. (Berkeley)
Max Planck Institute for Innovation and Competition

Prof. Dr. Michael Kort
University of Augsburg

Prof. Dr. Thomas M.J. Möllers
University of Augsburg

Prof. Dr. Dres. h.c. Joseph Straus
Max Planck Institute for Innovation and Competition

Volume 36

Nadiya Farah

# Harmful Trademarks

Towards a New Understanding of Moral Bars
in GCC Registration

**Nomos**

MIPLC Munich   Augsburg
       **Intellectual** München
       **Property** Washington DC
       Law Center

**The Deutsche Nationalbibliothek** lists this publication in the
Deutsche Nationalbibliografie; detailed bibliographic data
are available on the Internet at http://dnb.d-nb.de

a.t.: Munich, Master Thesis Munich Intellectual Property Law Center, 2017

ISBN     978-3-8487-5283-6 (Print)
         978-3-8452-9456-8 (ePDF)


**British Library Cataloguing-in-Publication Data**
A catalogue record for this book is available from the British Library.

ISBN     978-3-8487-5283-6 (Print)
         978-3-8452-9456-8 (ePDF)


**Library of Congress Cataloging-in-Publication Data**
Farah, Nadiya
Harmful Trademarks
Towards a New Understanding of Moral Bars in GCC Registration
Nadiya Farah
103 pp.
Includes bibliographic references.

ISBN     978-3-8487-5283-6 (Print)
         978-3-8452-9456-8 (ePDF)


1st Edition 2019
© Nomos Verlagsgesellschaft, Baden-Baden, Germany 2019. Printed and bound in Germany.

# Abstract

This thesis examines how Arab Gulf states that have Islamic law as the main source of legislation and large expatriate communities, apply moral bars to trademark registration. It considers whether the particular social and moral norms in these Islamic countries lead to stricter standards being applied at the trademark offices and courts. The main research questions this thesis seeks to explore are: i) to what extent are immoral trademarks proceeding to registration in conservative Islamic countries that apply trademark law in conformity with Sharia, compared with Western jurisdictions, ii) what reasoning and principles are being employed to shape decisions, and iii) can a concept of 'harm' improve our understanding of the latent power of trademarks to normalise behaviour and therefore our understanding of the moral bar thresholds that states set. The thesis is in five parts. Chapter I discusses the main problems with efforts to prohibit trademarks that are contrary to morality or public order. Chapter II presents the theoretical and legal foundations of trademark law. Chapter III explores the foundations of the GCC trademark system and the role of the Shari'a (Islamic religious law). Chapter IV investigates the main reasons why countries apply moral bars to trademark registration and seeks to identify differences in the reasoning between the Gulf and Western jurisdictions. Chapter V illustrates a selection of cases of trademark rejections and interprets them in order to derive insights.

The thesis shows that moral bars operate differently and that trademark law is imbued with cultural norms; this implicitly supports the territoriality principle in intellectual property law.[1] The thesis also shows that a harm-based model offers a useful lens through which to consider the influence of trademarks on society. Further research is needed.

---

1 The principle of territoriality provides that IP rights are territorially limited, such that the scope of protection for right owners is the territory of the state granting the right. In considering the granting of the right and its scope, the national granting authority resorts to its own domestic requirements for protection, which are respected as a function of state sovereignty. Accordingly, members of the Madrid system in trademark law can still reject an International Registration under the particularities of their domestic law, such as on morality grounds.

# Table of Contents

# Acronyms and Abbreviations

| | |
|---|---|
| CJEU | Court of Justice of the European Union |
| ECHR | European Convention on Human Rights |
| ECtHR | European Court of Human Rights |
| EU | European Union |
| EUIPO | European Union Intellectual Property Office |
| GCC | Gulf Cooperation Council |
| IP | Intellectual Property |
| MA | Madrid Agreement |
| MENA | Middle East and North Africa |
| MP | Madrid Protocol |
| OHIM | Office for Harmonization in the Internal Market |
| TRIPS | Trade-Related Aspects of Intellectual Property Rights |
| UAE | United Arab Emirates |
| UKIPO | United Kingdom IP Office |
| U.S. | United States |
| USPTO | United States Patent and Trademark Office |
| WIPO | World Intellectual Property Organisation |

# Introduction

## 1. Background

Ever since a legal concept of 'trademark' began to emerge after 1860,[2] the law regulating trademarks has often been asked to define the contours of this 'brand' of property right. Modern day developments continue to raise the issue of the boundaries of trademark rights and the influence of signs and symbols on society. Terrorist attacks, political upheaval, revolutions, changing social and moral norms, public health challenges, discrimination, and inequities - all of these transformative events and unfortunate realities grow the market for new trademarks. Firms choose words, slogans, devices that tap into the current discourse. Ubiquitous social media puts more focus on the trademarks that do or do not make it onto the register.

Trademark protection is given for signs that are "capable of distinguishing the goods or services of one undertaking from those of other undertakings".[3] Trademarks that are contrary to morality or public order present an ongoing problem. Barring them from the register to protect public sensibilities and "religious, social or family values"[4] may come at the expense of fundamental liberties like free speech. Another problem is that morality is culturally circumscribed, which does not lend itself to legal consistency in trademark decisions. These issues have been extensively explored in judicial and academic commentary. There has been less discussion about how these problems manifest themselves in socially and morally conservative jurisdictions, such as GCC countries. Also lacking is a deeper, more meaningful discussion of the perceived detriment of immoral trademarks. This thesis attempts to make a start on these two areas.

---

2  Lionel Bently, 'The Making of Modern Trade Marks Law: The Construction of the Legal Concept of Trade Mark' (1860-80) in L. Bently, J. Davis, and C. Ginsburg (eds), 'Trade Marks and Brands' (Cambridge University Press 2008), 3-41.

3  The Agreement on Trade-Related Aspects of Intellectual Property Rights (TRIPS agreement), Article 15(1).

4  Ghazilian's Trade Mark Application [2002] R.P.C. 33, [21].

## 2. Scope and geographical focus

The aim of this thesis is to analyse how the moral bar to trademark registration is applied in the GCC and the impact of Islamic law in this regard. It also maps out current classifications for immoral trademarks and proposes an alternative way of viewing the area, based on the concept of harmful trademarks. In exploring the notion of 'harm', there is an underlying premise that along with the benefits of trademarks, trademarks have the potential to lead to socially detrimental outcomes. Indeed, some have argued that a proliferation of offensive or exploitative trademarks can instigate or perpetuate alienation, and normalise harmful narratives.

The terrain is the Gulf countries and the units of analysis are three member countries: the United Arab Emirates, the State of Qatar, and the Kingdom of Saudi Arabia (henceforth UAE, Qatar, Saudi Arabia). They are chosen because they represent a spectrum of gradation in conservatism. Case law indicates that the gradations among them might hinder effective regional harmonisation of trademark laws under the new transnational GCC Trademark Law. The analysis includes European and U.S. regulation of trademarks for jurisdictional comparison. This means that cultural divergence will be illustrated on two levels: among the GCC countries and between the GCC bloc and the West.

## 3. Legal focus

The legal basis of this thesis is the optional moral exclusion under Article 6quinquies (B)(iii) of the Paris Convention, which states that trademarks that are "contrary to morality or public order" can be refused registration or cancelled.[5]

---

5 Paris Convention for the Protection of Industrial Property (1883), available at: www.wipo.int/treaties/en/text.jsp?file_id=288514

## 4. Methodology

This is a legal and ethnographic study, and positivist in approach.[6] Data collection is through trademark databases,[7] review of academic and judicial literature, and surveys of five law firms in Dubai, Doha and Riyadh. The literature reviewed includes trademark law, legal and religious texts, semiotics, and the power of brands. The robustness of survey results relies upon respondents having been sufficiently introspective to be able to relate their experience to the questions and to describe their experiences.

## 5. Chapter outline

Chapter I discusses commonly articulated problems of moral exclusions applied to trademarks. It is positioned as the opening chapter to bring the pervasive issues to the forefront at the outset, which frames the paper. The discussion shows there are countervailing interests of the state, traders and consumers, and these are difficult to balance. The concept of harm is introduced as a way to better understand the standard applied to moral bars in the Islamic countries of the GCC. Chapter II sets out the sources of trademark law and the rights and obligations that countries have in regulating trademarks. It considers the functions of trademarks and the benefits of registration, before then introducing the idea of moral bars that threaten these benefits. Chapter III presents the foundations of the GCC trademark system and discusses recent developments. Two exclusions that are largely unique to the GCC region are: a bar on trademarks associated with goods and services that are illegal or immoral under Shari'a law, and a political bar on trademarks from countries under sanction or embargo. With regard to the former, the chapter presents types of products that cannot be trademarked in the Gulf. It is apparent that there are more- and less-obvious ones. A comparison of how other jurisdictions deal with unlawful goods is offered. Chapter IV compares and contrasts rationales that underlie trade-

---

6  The proposed harm-based classification scheme/taxonomy in Chapter V and discussion of collective harm due to a proliferation of certain trademarks (e.g. pornographic, misogynistic) in Chapter I (A), may justify a normative analytical approach, however, the taxonomy should be seen strictly as a 'capture' tool, casting a wider net over contemporary trademark practice and social concerns across jurisdictions. Regarding the proliferation/accumulation argument, it is particularly conducive to future normative research.

7  EUIPO, UKIPO, TMVIEW, USPTO, WIPO Global brands database.

mark rejections in the Gulf, with those of the UK/EU and the US. Chapter V elucidates, through case-law examples, the thresholds of the moral bars applied in the three jurisdictions of this paper. Building on the discussion of harm, an alternative (jurisdiction-agnostic) taxonomy is presented.

# I. Challenges of regulating immoral trademarks

## Introduction

This chapter considers the tensions with applying moral bars to exclude certain trademarks from the register. Part A introduces the idea of 'harm' as an alternative conceptualisation of trademark regulation issues. As such, it offers a framework for exploring the case for intervention. Part B considers the extent to which (intervention on the basis of) moral exclusions constitute appropriation of intellectual property rights or curtail civil liberties, namely freedom of expression. Depending on the constitutional guarantees within a jurisdiction, trademark owners may challenge '*intrinsic*'[8] limits to trademark protection using appropriation of property arguments or freedom of expression arguments. Part C argues that legal certainty in the trademark registration process is compromised, as evidenced by inconsistent decisions.

## A. A concept of harm

*Harm as a more constructive characterisation.* This thesis explores the concept of 'harm' as a more constructive characterisation of the public interest issue for moral exclusions to trademark protection. 'Harm' has been raised or alluded to, in judicial discussion of offensive trademarks[9] but it is not dissected and it is often conflated with intangible descriptors like 'vulgar' or 'obscene'. To say that a trademark is objectionable because it is vulgar is an incomplete claim. Framing the problem from the perspective of 'harm' goes further in seeking to explain the root of the objection; i.e. what type of harm might flow from the mark or the accumulation of marks. A conceptualisation focused on the nature and substantiality of the harm, may also better serve traders because moral norms diverge between cultures and

---

8  Alison Firth, Gary Lea, and Peter Cornford, *Trade Marks - Law and Practice* (3rd edn, LexisNexis Butterworths, 2012) 78.
9  Case O-021-05 *Basic Trademark SA's Trade Mark Application* [2005] RPC 25; Case R 111/2002-4 *Dick Lexic Ltd's Application* [2005] ETMR 99 (see n 206).

over time.[10] One culture can be disturbed by the morals and practices of another. It is theorised that conservative Islamic countries are motivated to erect moral bars and set a low threshold for restriction of (brand) rights in order to *prevent* harm to society and preserve a status quo.[11] This goal, driven by Shari'a, dwarfs other countervailing interests. Indeed, there is no desire to let the market decide if use is prohibited.[12] Conversely, Anglo-American jurisdictions seek to *mitigate* harm because a balance is struck with speech rights, autonomy and other longstanding, founding principles. "THE SLANTS" case is an illustration.[13]

In criminal law, the 'harm principle' is used to determine what behaviour should be criminalised. The classic formulation of the harm principle is by John Stuart Mill: "The only purpose for which power can rightfully be exercised over any member of a civilised community against his will is to prevent harm to others... As soon as any part of a person's conduct affects prejudicially the interests of others, society has jurisdiction over it, and the question whether the general welfare will or will not be promoted by interfering with it, becomes open to discussion."[14]

In keeping with Mill's formulation, Simester and von Hirsch articulate: "the state is justified in intervening coercively to regulate conduct only when that conduct causes or risks harm to others".[15] Just as a harm principle is used as a guide to criminalisation, one may ask whether it can also be used as a guide to regulation of offensive trademarks that may cause or risk 'harm'. The important question for trademark regulation is not just what types of harm offensive trademarks can cause to society, if any, but what types of harm justify lawful intervention.

*The traditional approach to harm in trademark law.* A concept of harm has been applied in the context of expanding trademark protection beyond directly competing goods i.e. to non-competing uses. Historically, the harm was conceived as improper diversion of trade, caused by 'source of origin confusion' stemming from third party use of a mark. This concept of harm

---

10  See Chapter II(C)(III) for discussion on the terminology. Regarding changing norms, see Chapter 1(C) discussion of temporal and spatial inconsistency.

11  The discussion of thresholds is woven throughout this paper, see Chapter II(C)(2), Chapter IV(A)(1), Chapter V.

12  Peter W. Hansen, *Intellectual Property Law and Practice of the United Arab Emirates* (Oxford University Press 2009) 89. (See also infra n 43).

13  Infra n74.

14  John Stuart Mill, *On Liberty* (J. W. Parker and Son 1859).

15  A P Simester and Andreas von Hirsch, *Crimes, Harms, and Wrongs: On the Principles of Criminalisation* (Hart Publishing 2011) Ch 3, 35.

expanded from source of origin confusion to confusion over whether the owner was affiliated with or endorsed the infringer's use. [16]

The idea that intellectual property, including trademarks, can be harmful to society is not new. In the UK appeal of the rejection of "JESUS" as a trademark, Appointed Person Geoffrey Hobbs Q.C. defined antisocial trademarks as having an "ability to undermine an accepted social and religious value to a significant extent".[17] Scassa's discussion of antisocial trademarks alludes to a concept of harm; the catch-all term "antisocial marks" takes the Oxford English Dictionary definition of antisocial: "against the basic principles of society; harmful to the welfare of the people generally."[18] Patent law has long recognised the negative externality of antisocial behaviour. The morality and public order exclusion is found in patent law, notably the Biotechnology Directive Article 6(2), with its provisions recognised in the European Patent Convention (EPC) Article 53(a)/Rule 28.[19] The UK Patents Act 1977 used to refer to the power of an invention to "encourage" certain undesirable behaviour, including antisocial.[20]

*Defining harm.* Harm, in a strict sense, relates to the tangible 'loss' that flows from the trademark. In this sense, it is more than injury or affront to feelings or sensitivities. A trademark that incites the public to terrorist behaviour or hooliganism can be conceived as directly harmful. Direct harm should threaten to create a more tangible injury, a 'consequential' harm. Trademarks that create shock or disgust but don't have this persuasive element or link to behaviour, can be said to cause injury to feelings. This is a subtler, more indirect manifestation. Nevertheless, to the extent that it is an assault on the mind and sense of personal dignity, a harm argument could be made. This raises the question of whether 'tangibility' is the proper measure of harm.

*Harm to collective society (negative externalities).* It is suggested that there is a 'collective' or 'aggregate' aspect to harm. Having a few occasional drinks may be harmless, but when there emerges a binge-drinking culture and public health consequences ensue, the "collective marketplace" is harmed and restrictive measures may be applied by the state. The tobacco

---

16  Mark P. McKenna, 'Testing Modern Trademark Law's Theory of Harm' (2009) 95 Iowa Law Review 76-78.

17  *Basic Trademark* (n 9).

18  Teresa Scassa, 'Antisocial Trademarks', (2013) 103(5) The Trademark Reporter 1172-1213.

19  Article 53(a) EPC uses the term "ordre public".

20  Patents Act 1977 Section 1(3)(a). The Singaporean Patent Act Article 13(3) was identically worded.

plain packaging legislation undoubtedly ascribes to this view. Pornography is legal in some societies and illegal in others. It is hard to dispute that pornography has crept into the larger social construct of womanhood,[21] promoting the objectification of women and normalising a sexualised and subordinate view of them. A connection could be made between the growing prevalence of pornography and rape culture. All symbols, imagery, and narratives have a role to play.[22] There is harm to the collective society. In economic terms, there are 'negative externalities'.[23] Societies regulate against these external costs in different ways. Fershtman et al., in their discussion of taboos, describe three types of incentives that govern behaviour: private rewards, social incentives, and legal incentives.[24]

Snow argues that the purpose of protecting goodwill is to promote the "collective marketplace".[25] If protecting a producer's goodwill damages the collective marketplace, protection should be denied. Wasserman may be considering the 'collective marketplace' in relation to marks that promote prostitution.[26] The US represents a particular challenge here since free speech and 'viewpoint neutrality' are cemented in U.S. trademark law. [27]

*'Remote' harms.* In considering harm to society, 'remote harm' is relevant.[28] According to Simester and von Hirsch, some harms can be "remote in the sense that they involve certain kinds of contingencies" (on the conduct of others): abstract endangerment, accumulative harms and intervening choices.[29] 'Intervening choices' and 'accumulative harms' are relevant to 'antisocial' trademarks.

---

21  Twentieth Century French Philosopher and existential feminist Simone de Beauvior believed that our understanding of womanhood was a social construct.
22  See David Israel Wasserman, 'Trading Sex, Marking Bodies: Pornographic Trademarks and the Lanham Act' (2010) 23(121) National Black Law Journal, 6.
23  By-products of activities that damage the well-being of people or the environment.
24  Chaim Fershtman, Uri Gneezy, and Moshe Hoffman, 'Taboos and Identity: Considering the Unthinkable' (2011) 3(2) American Economic Journal: Microeconomics, 139, 142.
25  Ned Snow, 'Free Speech & Disparaging Trademarks' (2016) 57 Boston College Law Review, 1675.
26  Wasserman (n 22).
27  Snow (n25) at footnote 205, See also discussion of viewpoint neutrality in relation to the SLANTS case in Chapter IV of this paper.
28  It should be noted that the concept of 'remote harm' is founded on criminalisation of behaviour.
29  Simester and von Hirsch (n15) 57.

'Intervening choices' asks what role a person plays in the conduct of others. In trademark terms, one can ask what role an antisocial brand message has in inciting criminal or other highly offensive behaviour. Duff and Marshall analyse the consequences of recognising a "civic responsibility to attend not merely to the harms that our conduct might directly cause to others, but to at least some of the ways in which it might facilitate the commission of harm by others."[30] Applying this type of remote harm to trademarks, regulation of antisocial trademarks is justified on the basis of a causal link between the trademark and behaviour. Equally, however, it could be opposed on the ground that it is difficult to establish causality in the case of intangible property. This leaves harms arising from "inciting trademarks"[31] as merely an assumed harm.

'Accumulative harm' considers the threshold at which intervention is warranted; in other words, at what point is the harm deemed significant. This is relevant to the proliferation of inappropriate trademarks argument. It follows that the issue of remote harm and trademark regulation merits further exploration, which is not possible within the bounds of this paper.

*The power of trademarks.* Commentators agree that trademarks have gradually expanded from their primary quality and source identifying functions, as enumerated and protected in trademark legislation and case-law, and transformed into something more symbolic and socially powerful. Modern trademarks are carriers of speech. They are "constituent building blocks of social identity and convey political, social or emotive speech."[32] Indeed, Wasserman discusses trademarks that perpetuate sexual and racial subordination.[33] As such, today "the trademark is the message."[34]

Trademarks can also be politically powerful and jarring. Brands, images and symbols have the power to embrace political positions or express political messages. Highly subversive brand messages could raise public order objections. One might consider marks and slogans associated with campaigns to unseat sitting governments, or that are potentially extremely divi-

---

30  Robin A. Duff and S.E. Marshall, "Abstract Endangerment', Two Harm Principles, and Two Routes to Criminalisation' (2015) 3(2) Bergen Journal of Criminal Law and Criminal Justice 131-161.

31  See harm classification scheme in Chapter V.

32  Llewellyn Joseph Gibbons, 'Trademarking the Immoral and the Scandalous: Section 2(a) of the Lanham Act' in Peter K. Yu (ed), *Intellectual Property and Information Wealth: Issues and Practices in the Digital Age* (Volume 3, Ch 4, Praeger Publishers 2007).

33  Wasserman (n 22).

34  Gibbons (n 32) 112, (citing - author unknown).

sive. An application to register JE SUIS CHARLIE following the terrorist attack on the offices of French newspaper Charlie Hebdo, was rejected by the EUIPO on public interest grounds.[35] Gerhardt argues strongly for brands as powerful tools of political expression.[36] She postulates that entrepreneurial brand owners, in times of public mistrust in the political system especially, can and should leverage the expressive value of trademarks. "Trademarks... can be effective entrepreneurial tools in disrupting political entrenchment." But it does not have to be the brand owners; politics and symbols are also crossing over in the design world. "Bootlegging" sees fashion companies repurpose brands to deliver a subversive message. The Victoria & Albert Museum in the UK recently acquired a t-shirt design featuring the word "Corbyn" above a Nike swoosh.[37] Indeed, trademarks that are seen as conveyers of political messages are considered particularly harmful by states with lower tolerance for disunity and dissidence.

## B. Appropriation of trademarks

*Whether trademarks are positive or negative rights.* The authority of public bodies to interfere with trademark rights is connected to whether trademark law grants a positive or negative right. A "negative" or "static" right is a right to exclude third parties from exploiting the registered trademark. A "positive" right is a use right. A literal reading of the language of Article 16(1) of the TRIPS Agreement suggests a registered trademark offers the proprietor no more than a blocking right: "The owner of a registered trademark shall have the exclusive right to prevent all third parties not having the owner's consent from using in the course of trade identical or similar signs for goods or services which are identical or similar to those in respect of which the trademark is registered where such use would result in a likelihood of confusion."[38]

The conventional view is that trademark registration is solely a negative right to exclude. It has been so held in cases across jurisdictions: *BAT v Aus-*

---

35 "Je suis Charlie" Trade Mark Application 1668521.

36 Deborah M. Gerhardt, 'Trademarks as entrepreneurial change agents for legal reform' (2017) 95 North Carolina Law Review 1481, 1523.

37 Jeremy Corbyn, is current leader of the UK Labour party and the Opposition. He unexpectedly won huge gains in parliament to become leader.

38 See article 16(1) TRIPS. Additional protection for well-known marks is established in Article 16(2) and 16(3) of TRIPS and Article 6bis of the Paris Convention

*tralia, Anheuser-Busch Inc. v Balducci*, and the WTO Panel report in *EC-Trademarks and GIs*.[39] It is explained by academics including Bonadio, Nuno Pires de Carvalho, and Landes & Posner.[40] According to Landes & Posner, "[A] property right is a legally enforceable power to exclude others from using a resource, without the need to contract with them". Cohen offers a succinct conceptualisation of the exclusionary element as: "To the world: Keep off X unless you have my permission, which I may grant or withhold. Signed: private citizen. Endorsed: The state".[41] In Anglo-American jurisdictions, the state's lack of 'endorsement' has no bearing on continued use of the unregistered trademark by the trader.[42] In the GCC, however, use of an unregistrable mark is a criminal offence.[43] Evans and Bosland note that TRIPS imposes minimum requirements and that domestic laws can grant a positive right.[44] Article 17(2) of the GCC Trademark law states: "The owner of a registered trademark shall have the exclusive

---

39  *British Am. Tobacco Australasia Ltd & Ors v. Commonwealth of Australia, [2012] HCA 43*, available at: www.austlii.edu.au/au/cases/cth/HCA/2012/43.html, Justice Crennan considered that the positive right was relegated to "ancillary" status relative to the negative right [248], while Chief Justice French raised the spectre of lawful loss of rights by non-renewal and actions such as cancellation/revocation [31]; although note dissent by Justice Heydon who considered tobacco brand restrictions a suppression of intellectual property rights because trademarks represent a "legally endorsed concentration of power over things and resources" that rest with the owner [218]; *Anheuser-Busch Inc. v Balducci Publications 28 F 3d 769 at 777 (8th Cir 1994)*; Panel Report, *European Communities - Protection of Trademarks and Geographical Indications for Agricultural Products and Foodstuffs*, Complaint by Australia, WTO - DS290; U.S. case *Anheuser-Busch Inc. v. Balducci Publ'ns, 28 F.3d 769, 777 (8th Cir. 1994)*.

40  Enrico Bonadio, 'Bans and Restrictions on the Use of Trade Marks and Consumers' Health' (2014) 4 Intellectual Property Quarterly 326-345; Nuno Pires de Carvalho, The TRIPS Regime of Trademarks and Designs (Kluwer, 2011, second edition, 343); Alberto Alemanno and Enrico Bonadio, assert that "...no positive right to use trademarks is offered by TRIPS to trade mark holders" ('Do you Mind my Smoking? Plain Packaging of Cigarettes under the TRIPS Agreement', J.Marshall Rev. Intell. Prop. L. 450, 462 (2011)).

41  Felix S. Cohen, 'Dialogue on Private Property' (1954), IX Rutgers Law Review 357.

42  Note, for example, the Supplemental Register and protection of common law trademarks subject to use, in the U.S.

43  Hansen (n 12).

44  Simon Evans and Jason Bosland, 'Plain Packaging of Cigarettes and Constitutional Property Right' in Public Health and Plain Packaging of Cigarettes - Legal Issues, Ch 4, 53.

right to use its mark and to prevent third parties from using its mark…"[45] [46]However, in practice only the negative right is recognised.[47]

## 1. Are trademarks property?

Trademarks are a form of property.[48] [49]They fall within the body of 'property' protected by the European Convention on Human Rights (ECHR) and the Charter of Fundamental Rights of the European Union (CFR).[50] The first recorded Federal infringement case in the U.S. was in 1844.[51] In the UK, a property right in trademarks was first recognised by the Chancery Court in 1863.[52] However, some decry the recent expansion of this property right, for example, where an infringement cause of action can be based on confusion for non-competing goods (e.g. dilution).[53] Furthermore, as has been discussed, the integrity and bounds of the trademark right has been tested by state legislation in Australia (and ensuing case law)[54] and the UK, restricting brands on tobacco packaging. In a similar vein, Cohen's reference to 'state endorsement' and the majority position in *BAT v. Australia* look rather like deference to a margin of state discretion with regard to this property right. Setting aside the question of the legitimacy of State interference with trademark "use", the acquirable right itself is certainly a

---

45  Trademarks Law of the Gulf Cooperation Council (GCC) (English translation. The Arabic version is the definitive legal text), issued by law no. 6 of 2014.
46  Right to use/exploit: Bahrain Article 15; Oman Article 39(1) Industrial Property Rights Law (promulgated by the Royal Decree No. 67/2008).
47  Jon Parker 'The GCC Trade Mark Law', Gowling WLG, (IIPLA Presentation 2017).
48  Michael Spence, 'The Mark as Expression/The Mark as Property' (2005), 58 Current Legal Problems, 493, citing the UK Trade Marks Act 1994 section 22.
49  Proponent of property in the subject matter: J Harris, 'Property and Justice' (1996); Proponent of property in the right to control use of the subject matter: Spence ibid 494-495.
50  *Anheuser-Busch Inc. v Portugal* espoused the right to own property under Article 17(1), (2), of the European Charter of Fundamental Rights and Freedoms.
51  See Chapter II (A) for more detail on the development of a property right in trademark.
52  *Leather Cloth Company v. American Leather Cloth Company* (1863), cited by Frank I. Schechter (See n 110).
53  Michael Spence, 'The Mark as Expression/The Mark as Property' (2005), 58 Current Legal Problems, 491, 493.
54  See n 39.

transient one[55] because it is a construction; it may be lost by non-renewal or non-use in most jurisdictions, including the US, EU, and GCC.[56]

Trademark legislation represents a delicate balance between private (traders) and public (consumers) interests.[57] Some judges have articulated that trademark rights are a particular species of property right that is subservient to the public interest.[58] But the right of a state, having granted a trademark right, to then restrict the owner's (not third parties') use of it in furtherance of the public interest, is controversial. The charge of unjustified expropriation of investment and IP has led to investor-state arbitration at the WTO. The issue has plagued the aforementioned tobacco control legislation ('plain packaging') that seeks to prescribe the appearance of tobacco packaging, including how trademarks appear on the packaging. Similar restrictions are being considered for the alcohol and junk food industries.

## 2. Are trademarks tools of expression?

The right to freedom of expression is guaranteed in many state constitutions and in human rights treaties.[59] In countries like Australia or the GCC states, trademark owners are less likely to base a challenge to moral bars or health-based restrictions, on freedom of expression grounds: Australia's Constitution does not protect the freedom of expression either expressly, or for non-political issues even impliedly.[60] In Europe and the US, strong protections are afforded to certain fundamental freedoms and rights. GCC

---

55  Mark D. Davison, Ian Horak, The Hon. Justice William M. C. Gummow, 'Shanahan's Australian Law of Trade Marks and Passing Off' 5th ed, (2012): "the property in a statutory trade mark is not permanent", 78.

56  Chief Justice French (n 39). Note that the period of non-use in the GCC and EU is five years, cf. a three-year non-use period in the US.

57  See Gummow J in *BAT v. Australia* [68]; M.D. Pendleton, 'Exercising Consumer Protection - The Key to Reforming Trademark Law' (1992) 3 Australian Intellectual Property Journal 110, 111.

58  In *BAT v. Australia*, the Chief Justice stated that trademark rights were "instrumental in character", (n 39) [30].

59  Article 10, European Convention on Human Rights (freedom of expression); Article 11 Charter of Fundamental Rights of the European Union (freedom of expression and information); Amendment 1 of the U.S. Constitution. Some countries have stronger protection for freedom of expression than others.

60  In 1992, the High Court of Australia held there was an implied right to freedom of expression for public and political discussion.

countries may do so on paper,[61] but the institutions and mechanisms that allow for rights to be robustly enforced are lacking to varying degrees. In other countries, the relevant issue for trademark applicants is whether there is a free speech right to trademark registration and if so, what are the contours of such a right?

The modern premise is that a trademark *is* a form of expression/speech.[62] It is settled law that trademarks have a communicative function.[63] The US Federal Circuit, affirmed by the Supreme Court, has recently stated that trademarks are commercial speech.[64] European case law shows freedom of expression principles have been considered for some time.[65] Article 10 ECHR recognises freedom of expression: "everyone has the right to freedom of expression ... without interference by public authority." The right is to "receive and impart information and ideas without interference by public authority". It includes commercial expression, as held by the European Court of Human Rights (ECtHR) in *Casado Coco v. Spain*: "Article 10 (art. 10) does not apply solely to certain types of information or ideas or forms of expression...., in particular those of a political nature; it also encompasses...information of a commercial nature...".[66]Amendment 1 of the U.S. Constitution holds that "Congress shall make no law...... abridging the freedom of speech...".

Most EU states have incorporated the ECHR into their domestic law. States may derogate from ECHR provisions under the "margin of apprecia-

---

61  See Article 47 of Qatar's Constitution, Article 30 of UAE Constitution, and Article 39 of Saudi Arabia's constitution (Basic Law of Governance 1992). The texts are available at: https://wipolex.wipo.int/en/legislation/results?subjectMatters=20.

62  'Expression' is favoured in European discourse; 'Speech' is used in the U.S.

63  The seminal and controversial case on this is *L'Oréal v Bellure;* "Trademarks may become communicative symbols standing for something besides the source of sponsorship of the product in whose service they originated." For more on this see Chapter II(B)(2) (Trademark functions). See also Annette Kur, 'Trademarks function, Don't They? CJEU jurisprudence and Unfair Competition Principles' international review of industrial property and copyright law 45(4):434-454 · June 2014; Malla Pollack, 'Your Image Is My Image: When Advertising Dedicates Trademarks to the Public Domain-with an example from the Trademark Counterfeiting Act of 1984', (1993) 14 Cardozo L. Rev. 1391, 1393.

64  Freedom of expression concerns prevailed in THE SLANTS case.

65  Although note dissent from Judge Lourie in the Federal Circuit Court of Appeals, that trademarks are commercial speech.

66  *Casado Coco v. Spain*, 26 January 1994, Application No. 15450/89 [35], Series A. No 285, § 35ff,

tion" doctrine if the derogation is justifiable.[67] The assumption is that countries have better knowledge of their own political, social and cultural traditions than does the ECtHR. However, discretion is subject to ECtHR supervision, as established in *Handyside v UK*.[68] The case concerned the state's prima facie violation of Article 10 ECHR for the "protection of morals". Article 10 is a qualified not an absolute right. As such, a public authority can lawfully interfere with it if there is a "legitimate aim", if the interference is "necessary in a democratic society" (proportionate to the legitimate aim pursued), and if it is "prescribed by law". This built-in test is set out in Article 10(2)[69] and applied by the ECtHR to determine if an interference is unlawful. The margin of appreciation may be wide or narrow, depending on how far the Court scrutinises the legitimacy of the aims. ECtHR jurisprudence on Article 10 reveals that the Court, in applying the principle of proportionality, seeks to strike a fair balance between the demands of the European Union and the protection of fundamental rights.[70]

In considering registrability of a mark, U.S. and EU/UK cases often articulate the need to uphold the right to freedom of expression.[71] However, in EU/UK trademark case-law in particular, it is not clear how determinative the right is in any given judgment. Analysis of the principle has been too superficial to understand its role in the hierarchy of interests.

Whilst Europe holds that the right of free expression is not abridged by denial of registration,[72] the U.S. has recently departed from this position[73] in the 2017 Supreme Court decision in *Matal v. Tam* (at least with regard

---

67 However according to Bonadio (n 40), restrictions on trademark rights are not amenable to this type of justification because they're not positive rights.

68 *Handyside v The United Kingdom ECHR (5493/72, (1976) 1 EHRR 737).*

69 The right "may be subject to such formalities, conditions, restrictions or penalties as are **prescribed by law** and are **necessary in a democratic society**, in the interests of national security, territorial integrity or public safety, for the prevention of **disorder or crime**, for the protection of health or **morals**,.."

70 *Soering v United kingdom (1989) 11 EHRR 439*, [89] "inherent in the whole of the Convention is a search for a fair balance between the demands of the general interest of the community and the requirements of the protection of the individual's fundamental rights."

71 UKIPO cases: JESUS JUNKIE (0-133-10), JESUS (*Basic Trademark* (n 9), *Ghazilian's Trademark Application* (n 4) [6]-[7]; EUIPO cases: MECHANICAL APARTHEID (n 310), JESUS; US cases: *Harjo v Pro-Football* (REDSKINS), *In re Brunetti* (FUCT), *Matal v. Tam, 582 U.S. ___ (2017)* (THE SLANTS).

72 Case *T-417/10 Cortes del Valle Lopez v. OHIM* [26].

73 The precedent was set in *In Re McGinley.*

to disparaging marks).[74] Not everyone agrees; Ramsey argues that the speech right is superseded by the right of countries to exercise their discretion for morality and public order reasons and that, as with *Cortes del Valle Lopez v. OHIM*, as long as use of unregistered trademarks is permitted, there is no actionable harm to expression.[75] Baird warns, however, that there is a "defined public policy" to discourage the *use* of marks rejected under the US exclusion (s. 2(a) Lanham Act).[76] According to the logic that free speech is unharmed if use is allowed, trademark decisions in the Gulf would, in theory, accept more borderline marks since the trader could face criminal sanctions if he/she were to use it after it was rejected.[77] However, there is no indication that this is a consideration in examinations.[78]

## C. The uncertainty of legal certainty

Trademark laws banning registration of offensive marks have been criticised for reducing legal certainty. Legal certainty is a 'rule of law' principle to protect citizens from arbitrary government. It can be traced back to Aristotle (350BC), and Montesquieu who gave the idea modern expression.[79]

Rule of law is a modern constitutional preoccupation in democratic countries, and has particular significance in uncodified constitutions

---

74  An Asian-American band contested the USPTO's denial of registration of "The Slants" (an ostensibly racial slur) under the Lanham Act's Section 2 Disparagement clause. The USPTO based the rejection on "a substantial composite of persons" deeming the mark offensive. The TTAB upheld the decision and the case proceeded to the U.S. Court of Appeals for the Federal Circuit in *In Re Tam* (*In re Tam*, 808 F.3d 1321 (Fed. Cir. 2015) (en banc)). Sitting *en banc*, the Federal Circuit delivered a majority opinion that the Disparagement clause violated free speech and that registered trademarks constituted neither government speech nor government subsidy. Granting the USPTO's petition for certiorari, the Supreme Court ultimately affirmed the Federal Circuit 's decision and struck down the disparagement clause (*Matal v. Tam 582 U. S. ____ (2017)*) as unconstitutional under the First Amendment. The "scandalous and immoral" provision escaped scrutiny, thus the bar remains in place.

75  Lisa P. Ramsey, 'A Free Speech Right To Trademark Protection?' (2016) 106(1) Trademark Reporter 797.

76  Stephen R. Baird, 'Moral Intervention in the Trademark Arena: Banning the Registration of Scandalous and Immoral Trademarks' (1993) 83(5) Trademark Reporter 661, at 795 citing the Restatement of Torts § 629 (____ 1938).

77  Hansen (n 12). Trademarks denied on certain absolute grounds, cannot be used.

78  See Chapter IV.

79  Available at: https://plato.stanford.edu/entries/rule-of-law/

(common law) because there are no entrenched constitutional protections to individuals. In the rule of law context, the principle of legal certainty is often articulated as the need for the law to be 'clear, certain and prospective' so that citizens can regulate their conduct. Legal certainty is built into the ECHR under the "prescribed by law" condition for qualified and limited rights, since a law is, by definition, foreseeable and possesses sufficient legal certainty.[80] Allan links the rule of law to safeguarding individual liberties: "a crucial strand in the constitutional tapestry for the protection of liberty: it excludes arbitrary or discriminatory action by the powerful against the powerless by erecting the general law as a bulwark or barrier between the two."[81] Predictability encourages individuality and autonomy[82] and rational choices. The same sentiment is present in the Due Process Clause of the U.S. Fifth Amendment: "vague laws offend several important values. First, because we assume that man is free to steer between lawful and unlawful conduct, we insist that laws give the person of ordinary intelligence a reasonable opportunity to know what is prohibited, so that he may act accordingly."[83]

Unfortunately, potential trademark applicants cannot easily predict whether a given mark will fall foul of the moral exclusion or not. This is because examiners and judges while applying legal provisions, statutes and applicable guidelines, do consider the merits of each case. Statutes are subject to judicial interpretation. Examiners have to make an objective assessment of the trademark, but subjective judgement of statutory language is unavoidable,[84] notwithstanding that statutory language must not be too imprecise.[85]

---

80  Bonadio, (n 40) at n 79.
81  Trevor RS Allan, *The Sovereignty of Law, Freedom, Constitution and Common Law* (OUP 2013).
82  Denis J. Galligan, *Discretionary powers: A Legal Study of Official* Discretion (Clarendon Press 1986) 156.
83  The Fifth Amendment of the U.S. Constitution.
84  Baird (n 76).
85  The "void for vagueness" doctrine: Section 2(a) of the Lanham Act has been constitutionally challenged for violating due process guarantees of the Fifth Amendment, for being too vague to allow producers to predict the likelihood of obtaining registration. Baird (n 76) 679, citing *McGinley* case which was subsequently held to have been wrongly decided.

"Whilst these cases provide guidance on the way in which I must approach the issue, they also make it clear that the outcome of a case will depend upon its own particular facts"[86]

"...while the examination procedure must be as objective as possible and the examiners must strive, individually and collectively, to achieve the greatest possible consistency, it must be borne in mind that in each case the examiner enjoys a certain margin of discretion"[87]

"...while it is true that the Office must strive for consistency, each case must nevertheless be decided on its merits."[88]

This confirms there is a 'no-fettering-of-discretion' doctrine.[89] Discretion in the legal sphere is "autonomy in judgement and decision".[90] If discretion is unfettered, then decisions should show variation. Since variation can be predicted, even if ex-post, variation that has no discernible pattern may be termed 'inconsistency'. Inconsistency and legal certainty are inherently incompatible. In THE SLANTS case, the appellant accused the government of arbitrary and inconsistent decisions with respect to section 2(a). Farley has complained of "erratic and inconsistent" trademark decisions due to the subjectivity that comes with expression of ideas.[91] Carpenter and Murphy cite clearly conflicting results of the section 2(a) application.[92] Baird notes that the language of section 2(a), in fact, prescribes a subjective determination.[93] In Europe, the EUIPO has clarified when marks are to be rejected based on subjective values or objective criteria.[94]

---

86  *Case 0-330-05 FCUK* [31].

87  Second BOA in EASYPLAN- *Case R 109/1998-2* [18].

88  First Board of Appeal in Case R 192/2000-1 HOMES & PROPERTY.

89  Aldous J in MASTERMAN decision "discretion is unfettered, in the sense that it is not limited to any particular type of consideration but must be exercised on reasonable grounds."

90  Galligan (n 82) 8.

91  Ramsey (n 75), 808 citing Farley.

92  Megan M. Carpenter & Kathryn T. Murphy, 'Calling Bullshit on the Lanham Act: The 2 (a) Bar for Immoral, Scandalous, and Disparaging Marks' (2010) 49 U. Louisville L. Rev. 465, 482. Canada's clause 9(1)(j) has also been accused of being inconsistently applied. See commentary by Philip Lapin of Canadian firm Smart & Biggar, available at: www.lexology.com/library/detail.aspx?g=6216e725-7ec9-4cf a-9dad-75d87c1651b8.

93  Baird (n 76).

94  EUIPO 'Guidelines for Examination in the Office, Part B Examination, Section 4: Absolute grounds for refusal and European Union collective marks. Ch 7 "Trade marks contrary to public policy or morality, (Article 7(1)(f) EUTMR)" 5. The ap-

*Temporal and spatial inconsistency*. Changes in social and moral norms over time and space, introduce inconsistency in a temporal and a territorial (spatial) sense. Bonadio cites cases that have been decided differently a number of years later[95] and in different jurisdictions.[96] Trademarks that are 'merely distasteful' are not registrable in the UK and Europe, where the threshold for justifiable censure is real "outrage" and undermining values.[97] This differs from the United States' approach.[98] In the US., mere vulgarity is sufficient to bring the mark under the scope of Section 2(a) Lanham Act: BULLSHIT was held to be scandalous in 1981[99] and in 2006.[100] In the later office action, the examiner dismissed the idea that the word was any less profane simply because it was spoken more freely in contemporary American society. Fletcher and Kera's review of U.S. trademark decisions over forty-four years shows increasing tolerance, due to the inevitable subjectivity involved in judgment.[101]

Diverging decisions are also a feature of trademark law regulation in the GCC. The word mark CRIMINAL fell foul of the UAE's morality provision but was accepted in Bahrain, Kuwait, and Saudi Arabia.[102] Other types of objectionable marks also generate conflicting results in the GCC. Generic word marks QAHWATI ("my coffee"), ALLOOMAH ("a bit"), MAJNOON QAHWA ("crazy coffee") were registered in Qatar but denied registration in Saudi Arabia. However, there is arguably more legal certainty in the region because the examiners share the same religion, language, and culture. This is different from the large diversity among examiners in

---

95 Bonadio (n 40) 53. For instance, MECCA, HALLELUJAH.

96 ibid. For instance, JESUS was refused in the UK (*Basic Trademark* n 9), but accepted in Australia.

97 Ghazilian's Trademark Application (n 4); Fook Trade Mark Application O-182-05.

98 It is not clear where the SLANTS decision leaves this.

99 *Tinseltown Inc.*, *212 USPQ 863 (TTAB 1981)* - held scandalous for handbags and other personal accessories.

100 The energy drinks producer Red Bull attempted to register the mark BULLSHIT in the U.S. in 2006, but was rejected under Section 2(a) (*In re Red Bull GmbH*). This also illustrates spatial inconsistency as the company successful registered the trademark at the EUIPO.

101 Baird (n 76) at footnote 10, citing Anthony L. Fletcher and David J. Kera, 'The forty-Fourth Year of Administration of the Trademark Act of 1946' (1991) 81 TMR 601, 615: "The guidelines for determining whether a mark is scandalous or disparaging are somewhat vague and the determination is highly subjective."

102 It was ultimately accepted on appeal in the UAE.

proach is a function of whether the mark offends against policy or morality. See also Chapter II(C)(2) for discussion of the terms.

Western jurisdictions.[103] Regarding changing norms in the Gulf countries, there have been no significant changes in standards and values, but those who do point to changing social attitudes concede that trademark decisions are not changing accordingly.[104] Around fifteen years ago, however, Saudi Arabia agreed to accept trademarks depicting individuals or animals, which was previously prohibited.[105]

However, arguments against moral bars in trademark registration that are grounded in the value of legal certainty are not immune from challenge. Galligan, in his study of official discretion in modern legal systems, argues that: "consistency in decisions, while clearly important, is not to be regarded as the overriding concern."[106] Aldous J appeared to argue in the *Masterman* decision that guidelines should be treated as flexible rules. On guidelines, Galligan contributes that, while the generality of rules is necessary to ensure equality of a person's treatment, they may not fit cases that require individual treatment. Flexibility is needed to achieve larger goals.[107] Finally, key constitutional rule of law cases have overridden legal certainty in favour of a moral obligation to achieve fairness and justice based on modern social values.[108]

*Conclusion*

This chapter has explored some of the challenges of moral exclusion on trademark registration. It has shown that trademarks have been conceived as property and as vehicles of free speech. Therefore, applicants can raise freedom of expression or illegitimate appropriation of property arguments. However, the extent to which they can do so, depends partly on whether these rights are constitutionally recognised and enforced in a given juris-

---

103 Anne Gilson Lalonde & Jerome Gilson 'Trademarks laid bare: Marks that may be scandalous or immoral' (2011) Trademark Reporter 1476, 3. According to Lalonde and Gilson, decisions by the Trade Mark Office are "made by dozens of different individuals of varying political religious geographic and family backgrounds". The issue is compounded because previous registrations of similar marks are not regarded as precedential.
104 Survey responses.
105 Survey responses.
106 Galligan (n 82).
107 Trevor RS Allan, *Constitutional Justice: A Liberal Theory of the Rule of Law* (OUP 2001) 129.
108 *R v R, Shaw v DPP*.

diction. Both are contested concepts. The chapter has also shown that moral exclusions compromise legal certainty. The problem is potentially magnified in jurisdictions where decisions are not explained. A concept of harm was introduced; later chapters show that the GCC exhibits a lower harm threshold. This 'harm' is in the form of perceived decline in religious/family/social values, ultimately affecting the collective marketplace. Although this definition of harm (declining values) was present in *Ghazilian's Trademark Application*,[109] it is not a common argument in European case law.

---

109 In Ghazilian's Trademark Application (n 4), the Appointed Person Thorley Q.C. held that the sign TINY PENIS met the threshold for being denied registration because it went beyond mere distaste. To meet the threshold of 'justifiable censure' a mark should "provoke outrage" or "undermine current religious, family, or social values".

## II. The legal system for trademarks

### Introduction

This chapter maps the terrain of legal sources of trademark rights. Part A charts the path towards a property right in trademarks, a path forged largely by the courts. Part B outlines the legal sources of trademark rights. The sources of law include international IP treaties, national legislation and case law. Trademark functions are considered based on the premise that denial of trademark rights creates costs to producers in the form of benefits lost. Part C defines the different types of moral exclusions to trademark registration. It will establish that moral exclusions are ubiquitous across trademark regimes globally, but there is no uniformity in what a given moral exclusion means or in the thresholds for it to operate. Finally, it deconstructs prevailing terminology governing immoral trademarks and posits that there is a 'terminology problem'. It lays the foundation for an alternative taxonomy to address the terminology problem.[110]

### A. Development of trademark law

The Paris Convention for the Protection of Industrial Property of 1883 ('Paris Convention'), recognised the notion of a property right in a trademark. But even before this intellectual property treaty, some countries were already grappling with the issue.

*From 'merchant' and 'regulatory' marks to assets.* Schechter surveyed the development of trademarks, from the Middle Ages through to the modern and contemporary periods. His classical work showed that trademarks in the Middle Ages were 'merchants' and 'regulatory' marks. The cloth trades ushered in the concept of the trademark as an asset of value. The cutlery trades then established "property in trade marks as a legal possession." [111]

---

110  The alternative classification scheme is proposed in Chapter V. It is prefaced by part C.3 of Chapter II, which deconstructs existing terms in classifications in the literature and identifies limitations.

111  Frank I. Schechter, 'The Genesis of the Modern Law Relating to Trade-Marks' in Dinwoodie GB and Janis MD (eds), *Trade mark and Unfair Competition Law:*

Cases throughout the 17th Century saw marks being transmitted as assets though marriage and being bought and sold.

*From communication-based wrong to 'property' right.* From the sixteenth Century, England provided common law and equitable protection against misrepresentation in trade,[112] but protection was based on deceit rather than property.[113] [114] [115] [116] Stolte[117] recently identified Sandforth's *Case* (1584), displacing *Southern v How* (1618), as the oldest recorded trademark case in Anglo-American law. *Singleton v Bolton* (1783) was an action in law concerning medicines sold under another producer's mark. Other cases involving the protection of trademarks by law were *Day v Day* (1816) and *Sykes v Sykes* (1824).[118] In the courts of equity, *Blanchard v Hill* (1742) was a dispute between playing card merchants. Lord Hardwicke rejected the plaintiff's claim to a monopoly right to use his trademark "GREAT

---

*Themes and Theories (Critical Concepts in Intellectual Property Series* (Volume I, Edward Elgar Publishing 2014), and as reviewed by - G. Hyland, Columbia Legal Studies (2011). Schechter created the trademark dilution theory.

112  The path towards a property right in nineteenth century England, was complicated by the division of common law and equity courts prior to the Supreme Court of Judicature Act 1873. An action in law had narrow scope due to the need to prove fraudulent intent, cf. an action in equity at the Chancery court that required a misrepresentation likely to mislead. The benefit of an action in equity was injunctive relief, however if there was doubt about the legal right the case had to go to common law court first.

113  A showing of fraudulent use of the trademark was required. Schechter (n 110) clarifies that the plaintiffs/senior users of the marks were defrauded not deceived.

114  Bently (n 2) confirms that the law, up until 1860, was confined to misleading use of trademarks and specific trades. "[T]here was no such thing as a legal concept of 'trade mark' in 1860".

115  Lionel Bently, 'From Communication to Thing: Historical Aspects of the Conceptualisation of Trade Marks as Property' in Dinwoodie GB and Janis MD (eds), *Trademark Law and Theory: A Handbook of Contemporary Research* (Cheltenham: Edward Elgar Publishing 2008) 133.

116  ibid 143. In the period until 1875, case-law and legislative efforts (i.e. the failed 'Sheffield Act') signified that "[T]rade mark law started to be conceptualised as protecting a trade mark as an asset, rather than fixing on particular qualities of communicative act". The 'reconceptualisation' was later put on a statutory footing in the 1875 Trade Mark Registration Act which established a registration system.

117  Keith M Stolte, 'How Early Did Anglo-American Trade mark Law Begin? An Answer to Schechter's Conundrum' (1997) 8 Fordham Intellectual Property, Media and Entertainment Law Journal 505.

118  Ibid 138.

MOGUL" on playing cards.[119] Almost a century later in *Millington v Fox* (1838), Lord Cottenham granted equitable relief for trademark infringement. This was the first time that injunctive relief was granted in the courts of equity without evidence of intent to deceive.[120] Finally, in *Leather Cloth Company v. American Leather Cloth Company (1863)*, the Chancery court recognised a property right in trademarks.

Nevertheless, there remained throughout this time (19th Century) a fear, among lawyers, merchants and legislators on both sides of the Atlantic, of recognising trademarks as property.[121] The U.S. Congress, for example, considered the matter of trademarks to be trivial and left it to the individual States to handle: "justice can be had cheaper and faster in the State courts."[122] From the 1860s, a wave of trademark cases ensued, and the property right in trademarks began to be articulated.[123] Development of trademark accelerated in English and U.S. law, with the advent of the Industrial Revolution in the early twentieth century. In the U.S, the first recorded state infringement case was in 1837 and Federal case was in 1844.[124]

In the Middle East, the first reference of intellectual property was in relation to copyright protection.[125] Islamic law does not expressly entail protection of intellectual property. Where Shari'a law is silent, non-Shari'a legal norms are acceptable as long as they do not violate Shari'a principles.[126] In the UAE, IP laws began to be introduced in the early 1990s.[127] Saudi Arabia enacted its first trademark law in October 1939 (1358 Hijra).[128] Qatar introduced IP and trademark protection in the 1970s.[129]

---

119  Schechter (n 111) 134.
120  Bently (n 115) 4.
121  Schechter (n 110) 141. This was evident in the report of the Parliamentary Committee (1862), and in the debates of Congress (1870).
122  ibid.
123  Bently (n 115).
124  ibid.
125  Amir H. Khoury, 'Ancient and Islamic Sources of Intellectual Property Protection in the Middle East: A Focus on Trademarks (2003) 43(2) IDEA – The Journal of Law and Technology, 153.
126  ibid 162, (at footnote 46), citing Steven D. Jamar, The Protection of Intellectual Property Under Islamic Law, 21 Cap. U. L. Rev. 1079, 1081-82 (1993), 1082.
127  Hansen (n 12) 4.
128  Enacted by Royal Decree No. 33.1.4 of 24/6/1358H (October 1939). Bruce B. Palmer, 'Saudi Arabia's Trademark Law' (1986) 1(3) Arab Law Quarterly 323.
129  David Price, *The Development of Intellectual Property Regimes in the Arabian Gulf States. Infidels at the Gates* (Routledge 2012).

## B. Legal system

### 1. Sources of trademark law

Sources of trademark law can be grouped as follows: (1) treaties and regional agreements (supranational), (2) national statutes and subordinate legislation, (3) case law, (4) practice statements and rulings of regional and national trademark registries, (5) academic and professional commentary.[130]

Supra-national standards for trademark protection are set by the Paris Convention, the Agreement on Trade-Related Aspects of Intellectual Property Rights ('TRIPS'), and the Protocol Relating to the Madrid Agreement concerning the International Registration of Marks ('Madrid Protocol'). TRIPS is administered by the World Trade Organisation ('WTO') and sets minimum standards for certain IP rights, including trademarks.[131] There are currently 164 WTO members.[132]

### a) Paris Convention

Article 6 of the Paris Convention confers some discretion in matters of trademark registration upon contracting states. It sets out mandatory and optional grounds of refusal to register trademarks. It also specifies unlawful grounds of refusal. To summarise: Countries *must* deny registration to state emblems, official hallmarks, and emblems of intergovernmental organisations.[133] Countries *cannot* deny registration on the basis of a failure to register in the country of origin of the national citizen, or the nature of the goods to which the mark is applied.[134] There is no express mention of political sensitivities, such as trade embargos. Therefore, it will be assumed that this scenario (and, potentially, other scenarios not expressly treated),

---

130  This follows the categorisation of Jeremy Phillips in *Trade Mark Law, A Practical Anatomy* (OUP 2003), 3.05.

131  Pursuant to Article 1(1) TRIPS, WTO members enjoy some leeway in developing their national trademark laws but also restrictions: "Members may, but shall not be obliged to, implement in their law more extensive protection than is required by this Agreement…".

132  As of September 2017. See: https://www.wto.org/english/thewto_e/whatis_e/tif_e/org6_e.htm.

133  These are mandatory grounds of refusal (Article 6ter).

134  These are unlawful grounds of refusal, (Article 6(2)) and (Article 7) respectively.

may fall under the "public order" provision. Lastly, countries *may* deny registration on grounds pursuant to Article 6bis and Article *6quinquies* (B)(i)-(iii).[135] The main Paris provisions for this purpose of this paper are the optional moral exclusions under Article *6quinquies* (B)(iii) and, to a lesser extent, Article 7 (Article 15(4) TRIPS).

Trademarks that are "contrary to morality or public order" can be refused registration or cancelled under Article 6 *quinquies* (B)(iii) of the Paris Convention.

Article 7 is a restrictive provision: "The nature of the goods to which the trademark is to be applied shall in no case form an obstacle to the registration of the mark".[136] The provision applies to harmful but not illegal goods. Illegal goods can be lawfully excluded from the register. In the GCC, there is an absolute bar to certain Classes of goods and services that are contrary to Islamic morals: alcoholic beverages (Class 33), pork products (within Class 29), illegal activities and services like gambling, casinos, nightclubs (within Class 41). This is discussed further in later chapters.[137]

### b) National laws

With regard to domestic laws, the TRIPS Agreement determines the extent to which countries can circumscribe registration rights. Article 15(2) of the TRIPS Agreement allows states to deny registration to a trademark that constitutes protectable subject matter under Article 15(1), as long as the provisions of the Paris Convention (1967) are honoured.[138] States can also go beyond the Article *6quinquies* Paris Convention grounds of refusal.

Trademark matters also pertain to WTO Technical Barriers to Trade (TBT), TTIP IPR Chapter, and Bilateral investment treaties ("BITs"). With regard to 'BITs', because trademarks are IP rights, they are protected investments. As such, 'investors' can challenge state-imposed limitations that breach international IP treaties where there is an existing BIT.

---

135 Article *6quinquies* A(1) compels member countries to allow any trademark registered in the country of origin to obtain registration, unless an exemption ((B) (1)-(3)) applies.

136 It is recalled that this provision is an important point of contention in the Tobacco Plain Packaging cases.

137 See Chapter III.

138 Article 15(2) TRIPS Agreement states that WTO members are not restricted to the grounds of refusal in Article 15(1) TRIPS.

## 2. Trademark functions

Trademark law protects signs (confusion, double identity, unfair competition) and the functions of a trademark. The essential function of trademarks is to signal the *origin* of the goods and services for consumers.[139] Trademarks help consumers select goods by doing so. Frankfurter J called trademarks "a merchandising short-cut which induces a purchaser to select what he wants, or what he has been led to believe he wants".[140] In *L'Oréal*, the Court of Justice of the European Union (CJEU) recognised additional functions: guarantee of quality, communication, advertising or investment.[141] Swan et al. note that the modern trademark is more than an indicator of the source, it tempts the consumer to an experience through associations. It is a 'trust mark'.[142] This status as a 'trust mark' confers several secondary benefits on a brand, including allowing it to assume a position in the minds of potential consumers who then have an emotional reason to buy the brand.

In EU trademark law,[143] infringement of a trademark is subject to a condition that "the use must affect, or be liable to affect, one of the functions of the trademark". US trademark law considers the quality guarantee to be "the true function[s]".[144] It seems that the *L'Oréal v Bellure* theory of the essential function is 'consumer-focused' (prioritises lowering consumer search costs), while the US theory of quality guarantee is trademark 'owner-focused' (as Philips puts it, "bind[ing]" the owner).

## 3. Registering trademarks

Almost all countries that regulate the protection of trademarks operate a national registry (although neither Paris nor TRIPS mandate it). These registers are government agencies,[145] governed by national law and usually

---

139 *Arsenal Football Club plc v. Mathew Reed [2001] ETMR 860.*

140 Frankfurter J in *Mishawaka Rubber & Woolen Mfg. Co. v. S.S. Kresge Co* 316 U.S. 203, 205 (1942).

141 Case *C-487/07 L'Oréal SÁ v. Bellure NV [2009] ECR I-05185.*

142 Jerre B. Swann, Sr., 'The Trademark Reporter as Catalyst' (2011) 101(1) Trade mark Reporter, 88

143 Article 10(2)(a) Directive (EU) 2015/2436

144 Frank Schechter, 'The Rational Basis of Trade mark Protection' (1927) 40 Harvard Law Review, 813, 818.

145 See n 333-335.

connected to the patent or IP office.[146] An example of a regional trademark registry is the European Union IP Office (formerly OHIM) and the Benelux registry. The GCC has six national registries and no regional registry.

Article 6(1) of the Paris Convention makes the conditions for filing and registration of trademarks a matter for the domestic legislator. The U.S. and GCC countries examine absolute grounds of refusal and relative grounds *ex-officio*. The EUIPO examines on absolute grounds only, as does the UK, which rescinded relative examination through the Trade Marks (Relative Grounds) order, SI 2007/1976.[147]

*Opposition.* Unless successfully opposed, trademark protection ensues upon entry in the register. Renewal fees must be paid to prevent it from being cancelled. Conflict with prior rights is addressed in the opposition period. Here, an owner of a senior mark may file an opposition to prevent the acquisition of registration rights by a junior user.[148] In some jurisdictions, 'interested' third parties can file an opposition on grounds other than prior rights. In Europe, the main grounds for opposition are 'double identity' or 'likelihood of confusion'. Public order or immorality is only a cancellation ground (and absolute ground. See below, Part C.1). In contrast, in the U.S., an interested party can oppose the registration of a trademark they consider immoral, scandalous or disparaging in violation of section 2(a) of the Lanham Act[149] on the ground that its registration will cause them damage,[150] or injury.[151] In the GCC, any interested party can file an opposition on grounds such as fame and absolute grounds as per *Article 6ter* or Article *6quinquies* (B)(iii) of the Paris Convention. It is significant that in the context of opposition, trademark rights can be excluded before they come into existence.

---

146  Phillips (n 130), 43.
147  Section 5 Trade Marks Act 1994. Available at http://www.legislation.gov.uk/ukp ga/1994/26/section/5.
148  Publication in the official gazette initiates an opposition period: a third party can assert that they have prior rights and that the applied for mark is identical or confusingly similar. Not to be confused with cancellation proceedings.
149  Other grounds include abandonment of the mark; fraud; dilution.
150  Part A(3)(C), Trade mark Opposition Proceedings in the United States. Available at: http://www.wipo.int/export/sites/www/sct/en/comments/pdf/sct17/us_1. pdf.
151  Lynda Oswald, 'Challenging the Registration of Scandalous and Disparaging Marks under the Lanham Act: Who has Standing to Sue?' (2004) 41 American Bus. L. J. 251.

*Benefits of registration.* The main benefit to an owner of a registered trademark is exclusivity in the Class(es) in which it was registered. Additionally, registration acts as a warning to potential competitors that are already operating in that space. Competitors and courts are also guided by registered trademarks as competitors can invest in reliance on the mark's scope and courts can easily establish infringements.[152]

## C. Moral exclusions

### 1. Legal origins

Moral exclusions fall under absolute ground objections to trademark protection. They are *"intrinsic* limits"[153] or *'inherently'* objectionable.[154] Notwithstanding common law trademark rights in the U.S.,[155] common law protection in the UK (passing off) and some mixed systems such as in Germany, trademark rights are acquired through registration. The general rule for registrability is that the mark should be distinctive and not descriptive of the goods or services being sold/offered. A mark that meets the requirements can still be rejected per the exception in Article *6quinquies(B) (iii)* of the Paris Convention for marks that are "contrary to morality or public order".[156]

The parallel provisions to Article *6quinquies(B)(iii)* are Article 7(1)(f) of the European Union Trade Mark Regulation 2015/2424.[157] Article 3(1)(f) of the European Union Trade Marks Directive 2015/2436;[158] Article 3(3)(a)

---

152 *Myles Ltd's Application, case R711/199-3,5 December 2001 (OHIM),* [11].
153 Firth et al. (n 8).
154 Edward Smith, 'Absolute Grounds' paper submitted by United Kingdom for SCT Assistant Principal Hearing (2009). Available at http://www.wipo.int/expor t/sites/www/sct/en/comments/pdf/sct21/ref_uk.pdf
155 In the U.S., rights stem from use.
156 The exception was incorporated into the TRIPS Agreement by Article 2(1).
157 Regulation (EU) 2015/2424 of the European Parliament and of the Council of 16 December 2015 is an amendment to the Council Regulation that governs EU trademarks: the EU Community trade mark regulation (Council Regulation (EC) No 207/2009 of February 2009 on the Community trade mark [2009] OJ L 341/21). In addition to the EU CTMR, European trademarks are also governed by the Community Trade mark Implementing Regulation (2868/95).
158 Directive (EU) 2015/2436 is a recast of the 1989 Directive (2008/95/EC). Directive (EU) 2015/2436 approximates the laws of EU member states for national trademarks.

of the Trade Marks Act 1994 (UK); Section 2(a) of the Lanham Act (US); Article 3(2) of the GCC Trade Mark Law; Article 2(c) of the Law of Trade marks (Saudi Arabia); Article 8(2) (Qatar); Article 3(2) (UAE).

*The significance of linguistic variations in morality exclusions.* The wording of the exclusion varies across the written laws of different countries but is substantively the same. Language can differ, be supplemented, or be formulated more or less broadly. Linguistic variations provide a small window into the approach of a country towards this problematic category of marks.

At the European level, Article 7(1)(f) of Regulation 2015/2424 formulates the exclusion as "trademarks which are contrary to public policy or to accepted principles of morality." The EUIPO clarifies that 'morality' and 'public order' are different but overlapping concepts.[159] The Office also clarifies that the provision is formulated "very broad[ly]" and when interpreting it, the interests of traders and the public should be balanced. Section 3(3)(a) of the UK Trade Marks Act 1994, which implements Directive 2015/2436, follows this wording. Germany also refers to "accepted" principles.[160] It may be suggested that the inclusion of "accepted" signifies a dynamic element to social norms and attitudes. Indeed, Gibbons refers to a "pendulum", suggesting that the shifts can be bidirectional.[161] The Appointed Person in *Ghazilian's Trademark Application* remarked that "accepted principles of morality change with time."[162] France's Law 1991-7 employs the Paris Convention language,[163] as does the trademark law of Italy

---

159 EUIPO Guidelines (n 94).

160 World Trademark Review Yearbook 2017 - Trade mark procedures and strategies: Germany (Available at: http://www.worldtrade markreview.com/Intelligence/ Yearbook/2017/Country-chapters/Germany). German Trade mark Act, implements the Directive 89/104/EEC.

161 Llewellyn Joseph Gibbons (2005), 'Semiotics of the Scandalous and the Immoral and the Disparaging: Section 2(A) Trademark Law after Lawrence v. Texas' 9(2) Marquette Intellectual Property Law Review, 217.

162 Ghazilian's Trade Mark Application (n 4).

163 World Trademark Review Yearbook 2017 - Trade mark procedures and strategies: France (Available at: http://www.worldtrade markreview.com/Intelligence/Year-book/2017/Country-chapters/France). France implemented the first Directive 89/104/EEC (which uses "Accepted principles" Article 3(1)(f)) in its Law 1991-7. Article L711-3(b) of the Intellectual Property Code: Book VII. Trade marks, Service Marks and Other Distinctive Signs. Note that "Accepted principles" is used for designs (Article L511-7, BOOK V, Designs and Models), but not trademarks or patents.

and others.[164] Poland's trademark law contains a rather strong exclusion for marks that are "contrary to principles of social existence."[165]

Outside of Europe, Malaysia distinguishes scandal from offence, recognising a prohibition on registration for marks containing or comprising "scandalous or offensive matter or would otherwise not be entitled to protection by any court of law;"[166] Brazil's exclusion extends to respectability and honour, and alludes to disparagement against beliefs and members of religious cults. Unregistrable signs are those that are "contrary to morals and standards of respectability or that offend the honor or image of persons or attempt freedom of conscience, belief, religious cult or ideas and feelings worthy of respect and veneration."[167] The language comes quite close to that of the tort of defamation. There is no specific reference to public order but it may be covered, to some extent, by the listed freedoms (conscience, belief, religious cult). Chile bars "signs that are contrary to public order, morality and good behaviour, and the principles of fair competition and business ethics."[168] The U.S and Canada bar marks that are "scandalous, obscene or immoral."[169]

---

164  World Trademark Review Yearbook 2017 - Trade mark procedures and strategies: Italy. Available at: http://www.worldtrade markreview.com/Intelligence/Yearbook/2017/Country-chapters/Italy.

165  Phillips (n 129), 67.

166  Section 14(1)(b), Trade Marks Act 1976 (Act 175, incorporating all amendments up January 1, 2006)

167  Article 124(III) of the Law on Industrial Property (9,279/1996). Brazil's provision is broader than Paris, protecting personal respect and even personality rights, Article 124(III) prohibits signs that are contrary to "morals and standards of respectability or that offend the honor or image of persons or attempt freedom of conscience, belief, religious cult or ideas and feelings worthy of respect and veneration".

168  Chile's 'Industrial Property Law (19.039)' (September 30 1991. Modified by Law 19.996 (December 14 2005). Also governing Chile's trademark law is Law 20.160 (of January 2007. The law is regulated by Decree 236 of December 1 2005, modified by Economy Decree 36 of May 23 2012).

169  Canada - 'Trade marks Act', Article 9(1)(j); U.S. - Lanham Act, Section 2(a) (15 U.S.C. § 1052(a)), WTR Yearbook 2017 - Trade mark procedures and Strategies. Under section 2(a) of the Lanham Act the U.S. bars from the principle register, "immoral" or "scandalous" marks (and prior to "The Slants" Supreme Court decision, marks that may "disparage...persons, living or dead, institutions, beliefs or national symbols, or bring them into contempt, or disrepute").

Turning to the GCC, none of the six member states include the dynamic term "accepted" in their national trademark laws.[170] GCC and other Arab/Muslim majority countries, such as Egypt, Turkey, Algeria, Morocco, Iraq, Jordan, Libya, stay close to Paris Convention (quinquies B(iii)) language.[171] Many add a separate clause in relation to symbols with a religious character or specific logos, like Red Cross, Red Crescent.[172] Saudi Arabia goes further by referring to marks that "violate" religion. Lebanon prohibits trademarks that include "a word, signal or symbol which is revolutionary or in breach of the public order or sound and good discipline."[173]

---

170 Qatar - 'Law No. 9 of 2002 on Trademarks, Trade Names, Geographical Indications and Industrial Designs' Article 8(2) "Every expression, design or sign contrary to moral or public order"; Bahrain - 'Law No. (11) For the year 2006 on Trade marks' Article 3(B); UAE - 'Federal Law No. 37 of 1992 on Trade marks' (as amended by Law No. 19 of 2000 and Law No. 8 of 2002), Article 3(2); Saudi Arabia - 'Law of Trade marks' (promulgated by Royal Decree No. M/21 of 28 Jumada I 1423 [Hjjra]. Corresponds to August 7, 2002 in the Gregorian calendar), Article 2(c) "Any expression, sign or drawing inconsistent with public order or public morality"; Oman - 'Industrial Property Rights Law' (promulgated by the Royal Decree No. 67/2008), Article 38(4)(c)(3); UAE – 'Federal Law No. 37 of 1992 on Trademarks' (as amended by Law No. 19 of 2000 and Law No. 8 of 2002), Article 3(2) "Any mark breaching the public morals or violating the public order"

171 Egypt - Article 67, Law No. 82 of 2002 Pertaining to the Protection of Intellectual Property Rights; GCC - Trade mark Act of the Member States of the Cooperation Council for the Arab States of the Gulf Article 3(2); Turkey - Article 7(k), Decree-Law No.556 Pertaining to The Protection of Trade Marks, in force as from June 27, 1995; Sudan. ,The Trade marks Act (1969 Act No.8); Algeria - Article 7(4), Order (Act) No. 03-06 dated 19 Jumada I, 1424 corresponding to July 19, 2003 related to Trade marks; Morocco - Article 135(b), Law no. 17-97 on the protection on industrial property (as modified and supplemented by Law 31.05); Iraq - Article 5(2), Trade marks and Descriptions Law No. 21 Of 1957 (as amended by Coalition Provisional Authority Order Number 80, April 2004); Jordan - Article 8(6) Law No. 33 of 1952 on Trade marks amended by Law No. 34 of 1999 Amending the Trade marks Law; Libya - Article 5(b), Trade marks Law (No. 40 of 1956).

172 National laws (n 170), Qatar –Article 8(5); Saudi – Article 2(b); UAE – Articles 3(4), 3(5).

173 Article 71 (Laws and Systems of the Commercial and Industrial Property in Lebanon Resolution No. 2385, issued on January 17th, 1924, amended by the Law of 31 January 1946, Decree No. 245 of February 23rd, 1983. Law No. 152 / L R of July 19, 1939). Member of Paris as of September 1, 1924. Not yet WTO member or Madrid Protocol member.

Religious sensibilities are expressly protected by some countries, including Pakistan, Iran, and the UAE. Pakistan refers to morality[174] and to trademarks containing "scandalous design" that may "hurt the **religious sensibilities** of any class of citizen of Pakistan, per se, or in terms of **goods or services**...intended to be so registered".[175] Public policy is only invoked in relation to collective marks[176] and certification marks.[177] The Islamic Republic of Iran prohibits a mark "if it is contrary to Rules of **Sharia**, public order or morality."[178] Saudi Arabia's Law of Trade marks denies registration to "Any expression or sign or drawing **violating religion**, or which is identical or similar to a symbol of religious nature".[179] The UAE also covers protected religious symbols: "Logos of the Red Crescent or Red Cross",[180] and "Marks that are identical or similar to symbols having a purely religious character."[181] [182]

Some countries have added provisions relating to religious or tribal-based marks. Sudan prohibits marks that are "emblems of exclusively *religious, sectarian or tribal* organization" (Article 8(g)) or that portray "a religious or tribal leader or any sectarian significance." (Article 8(h)).[183] Iraq's trademark law was amended by the Coalition government (under the administration of U.S. L. Paul Bremer, Administrator, Coalition Provisional Authority) in April 2004.[184] The amended law prohibits marks identical with, or similar to, "the insignia of the Red Cross, Red Crescent, or Geneva Cross" (Article 5(4)), only a minor change from the previous language which included the "Red star". Absent from the Coalition-amended law is the Israeli boycott clause that had been Article 5(12).[185]

---

174  Ordinance No. XIX of 2001, Article 14(3)(c).
175  ibid Article 14(3)(b).
176  ibid Article 6(1)(b), 13(c)(ii)).
177  ibid Article 7(1)(a)(ii), 15(d)(ii)).
178  Patents, Industrial Designs and Trade marks Registration Act of the Islamic Republic of Iran (2008), Article 32(b), available at https://wipolex.wipo.int/en/legislation/details/7706.
179  The first Saudi Arabian trademark law was enacted by Royal Decree in 1984 and amended by the current trademark law of August 2002. Article 2 enumerates trademarks that cannot be registered.
180  UAE trademark law (n172) Article 3(4).
181  UAE trademark law (n172) Article 3(5).
182  Also see Libya Article 5(e), 5(f) and Bahrain Article 3(E), (F).
183  The Trade marks Act of 1969. The Republic of Sudan is a member of the Arab League.
184  CPA/ ORD/26 April 2004/80.
185  "Marks which the office of Israel boycott decides to be identical to or resembling on Israeli Mark, emblem or symbol". Articles 5(9)-5(12) suspended.

## 2. Understanding 'morality' and 'public order'

The meaning of 'morality and public order' remains to some extent an enigma. Morality has been defined in patent case law as "'the belief that some behavior is right and acceptable whereas other behavior is wrong, this belief being founded on the totality of the accepted norms which are deeply rooted in a particular culture".[186]

The meaning of 'public policy' has been discussed by commentators including Bodenhausen,[187] Lloyd,[188] Giorgio del Vecchio,[189] and the Appointed Person Richard Arnold QC[190] who in the appeal against a failed invalidity declaration against the trademark FCUK provides a comprehensive history.[191] The idea that conduct and laws might contravene public policy or morals has its origins in the civil law (*ius civile*) tradition of continental Europe.[192] In 19th century France (the "codification period"),[193] 'public policy' was incorporated into the *French Civil Code of 1804* (Code Napoleon) and later in the Italian and Spanish Civil Codes.[194] Public policy norms are contractually underogatable: "laws relating to public policy and morals cannot be derogated from by private agreements."[195] The civil law system bore the idea of public policy norms. These are "laws of manda-

---

186 T356/93 *PLANT GENETIC SYSTEMS/Glutamine synthetase inhibitors* [1995] EPOR 357.

187 Bodenhausen, 'Guide to the Application of the Paris Convention for the Protection of Industrial Property', as revised at Stockholm in 1967, 113-116. Available at ftp://ftp.wipo.int/pub/library/ebooks/wipopublications/wipo_pub_611(e).pdf.

188 Dennis Lloyd, *'Public Policy: A Comparative Study in English and French Law'* (London: Athlone Press, 1953), 27 (as cited by Marks and Betancourt, infra n 194).

189 'Los Principios generales del Derecho' (translated by Juan Ossorio Morales) (Barcelona: Bosch, 1979), 41.

190 In UK trademark disputes, the hearing officer's decision can be appealed to the appointed person or the High Court. The 'Appointed Person' is a senior IP lawyer appointed by the Ministry of Justice.

191 *French Connection Ltd., No. 2184549 v. Woodman, No. 81862, Dec. O-137-06 (May 17, 2006)*

192 Tony Marks and Julio Cesar Betancourt (2012). 'Rethinking public policy and alternative dispute resolution: negotiability, mediability and arbitrability', Arbitration 2012, 78(1), 19.

193 ibid at (footnote 13) citing Thomas Glyn, *An Historical introduction to Modern Civil Law* (Aldershot: Brookfield, 1999)

194 Article 12 Italian Civil Code (1865); Article 1255 Spanish Civil Code (1889).

195 Marks and Betancourt (n 192), referring to the French Civil Code of 1804.

tory application." They represent a State's priorities.[196] Public policy is an idiomatic translation of "order public" which was used in *Philips v Remington*.[197] The direct translation 'public policy' is more commonly used in trademark legislation.[198]

In the GCC, the terms have never been classified[199]and in practice, the terms are conflated.[200] No explanations or guidelines are known to exist for GCC examiners. In the U.S. public policy seems to be an umbrella concept for all marks that are immoral, scandalous, disparaging, contemptuous, disreputable, deceptive and suggestive of a false connection.[201] UK and European case law is replete with examples where this distinction has been articulated. Clarifications are provided in the UK Trade Marks Manual.[202] The EUIPO Examination Guidelines state that marks rejected due to "accepted principles of morality" are rejected based on an objective assessment of "subjective values",[203] while marks rejected based on policy are rejected by an assessment based on objective criteria. Under the EUIPO approach, morality is subjective (perceived by the relevant public as directly against the basic moral norms of society) and the standard is the reasonable consumer with average sensitivity and tolerance thresholds.[204] Policy is considered objectively to contradict the basic principles and fundamental values of the European political and social order. Nevertheless, the overall goal of applying moral exclusions to trademark protection is to protect the public, moral norms, and encroachments on human dignity.

Public policy was defined in *Indica* as "the body of all legal rules that are necessary for the functioning of a democratic society and the state of

---

196 Phillip Louis Landolt. *Modernised EC Competition Law in International Arbitration.* Ch 5, 6-21.
197 Richard Arnold QC (n 191) at [6], citing *Philips Electronics NV v Remington Consumer Products Ltd [1998[ RPC 283*, [310] lines 8-12; Marks and Betancourt (n 192) 2 (citing Denis Lloyd).
198 'Public order' is used in TRIPS Article 27(2) for patents and the Biotechnology Directive 98/44/EC Article 6(1), EPC 1973 Article 53(a).
199 Survey responses.
200 The examiners will usually cite both together, simply following the wording of the law (Survey response).
201 Baird (n 76) 795.
202 Available at: www.gov.uk/government/uploads/system/uploads/attachment_data /file/587937/Manual-of-trade-marks-practice.pdf.
203 EUIPO Trade Mark Guidelines, Ch 7, available at: https://euipo.europa.eu/ohim portal/en/trade-mark-guidelines-pdf.
204 Judgement of 09/03/2012, T-417/10 '¡Que buenu ye! Hijoputa', para.HIJOPUTA', (§ 21).

law".[205] It is a necessary condition that the sign itself, or the message it conveys, is prohibited in law. Thus, it turns on 'legality'.

The morality and public order prohibition relates to harm. In *Dick Lexic Ltd's Application*, the Board stated that the mark DICK & FANNY for Class 9, 16, and 25 goods, should not have been rejected by the examiner.[206] Among other reasons, this was because it did not go beyond a question of taste. In order to meet the threshold of the prohibition, the mark must 'transmit a message'. This looks like a harm argument. This statement also reinforces the idea discussed earlier that 'mere distaste' is insufficient in the EU and should not be legislated. This is a higher standard than the GCC in terms of what constitutes harm.[207]

3. Tackling the terminology

Terminology and taxonomy in this area is confusing (Figure 1). Scassa sets out three categories of antisocial trademarks: (**1**) trademarks that are inherently contrary to morality or public order, (**2**) trademarks that are rendered objectionable by association with the goods or services (**3**) trademarks having an antisocial brand message. She focuses on the second and third categories. Within the first category are five sub-categories.[208] Baird focuses on the Lanham Act § 2(a) and finds seven types of Scandalous mark.[209] Abdel-Khalik, also US focused, proposes six types of Scandalous mark.[210] The UK Trade Marks Manual reduces offensive marks that are 'contrary to public policy or to accepted principles of morality' into three categories: (**1**) criminal connotations,[211] (**2**) religious connotations,[212] and (**3**) explicit/taboo signs.[213] The Manual states that marks can offend against morality without offending public policy, but the reverse is not as often true. "The

---

205  INDICA 65572/00.

206  *Dick Lexic's Application* (n 9).

207  This difference in thresholds is covered further in chapter III, chapter IV(A)(1), and chapter V.

208  Scassa (n 18).

209  Baird (n 76).

210  Jasmine Abdel-khalik, 'Disparaging Trademarks: Who Matters' (2015) 20(2) Michigan Journal of Race and Law 288-319.

211  *To promote* illegal or otherwise offensive behaviour.

212  To *undermine* accepted religious value.

213  UK Trade Marks Manual, 165, available at: www.gov.uk/government/uploads/sy stem/uploads/attachment_data/file/587937/Manual-of-trade-marks-practice.pdf.

term "public policy" in section (3)(3)(a) is intended to deny protection to marks which could "induce public disorder, or increase the likelihood of criminal or other offensive behaviour." This statement shows that there is a harm element in public policy. The US 2017 Trade mark Manual Examining Procedure (TMEP) 1203.01 clarifies that 'scandalous' and 'immoral' have different dictionary definitions, but in case-law and legislative history the two are conflated and treated as synonyms. According to Baird, 'immorality' is the redundant term, as no case has relied solely upon that term to refuse a mark.[214]

---

214 Baird (n 76) 728. The same point is made in *In re McGinley*, 660 F.2d 481, 485 at footnote 6.

## Figure 1: Current classifications in the literature.[215]

**UK Trade marks Manual**

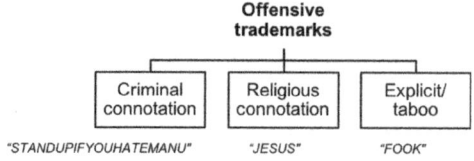

**Scassa**

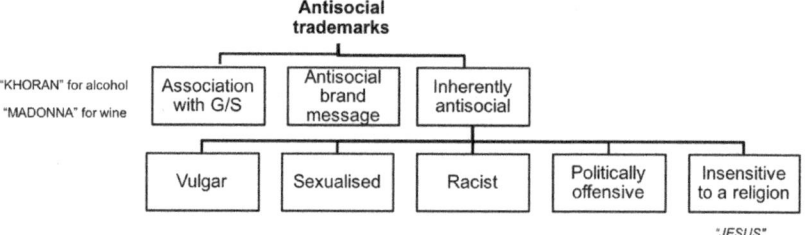

**Abdel-khalik**

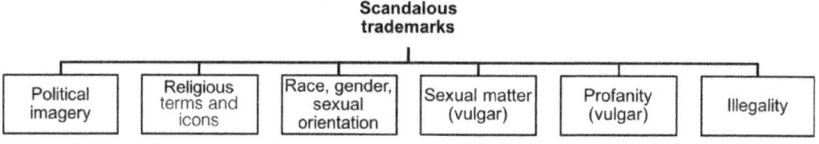

**Baird**

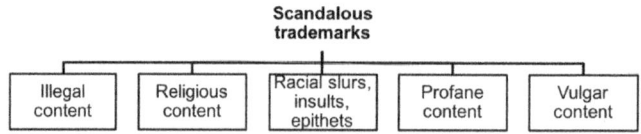

---

215 These classifications represent the understanding of the author of this thesis and may not be accurate.

*Advantages*. Scassa's classification is prescriptive for trademark practition-ers. It incorporates some of the 'methodological nuances' that practitioners will have to consider in order to derive the meaning, before deciding whether the meaning is offensive. Baird and Abdel-Khalik focus on "scan-dalousness". Their taxonomies are similar. Baird adds an 'innuendo' catego-ry, which is another methodological nuance. They all comprehensively classify the scenarios that could arise. The UK Trademarks Manual taxono-my facilitates a useful separation between marks likely to offend public policy on the one hand (criminal, religious marks) and marks relating more to principles of morality (explicit/taboo marks) on the other hand.

*Limitations?* In considering ways to leverage these classifications, it is im-portant to understand what logics should be present. The first logic is how the offensive meaning of the trademark is rendered: is it rendered literally, from an unambiguously vulgar word? Is it rendered by innuendo, such that the examiner has to put in extra effort? One can think of this as a 'methodological nuance', or even a 'pre-logic'. The second (and principal) logic is, what is the nature of the objection; in other words, why should this word be objected to (the nature of the harm)? This can be considered a 'substantive nuance' or 'interpretative nuance'.

There is room for improvement in four areas: [1] Some classifications combine elements from two different logics.[216] The logics may overlap in practice but conceptually they should be kept separate; [2] Most classifica-tions fail to reach behind descriptive labels that do not explain the "harm-fulness" of the mark;[217] [3] The taxonomies of Abdel-Khalik and the UK Trade marks Manual appear to contain a single logic, which is also insuffi-cient. Additionally, the UK classification fails to explicitly account for trademarks of a political nature or slurs against minority groups. These would have to be considered under 'explicit/taboo' or 'criminal connota-tion'.[218] Indeed, it has been argued that the last Western taboos are slurs against minority groups/individuals;[219] [4] Finally, none of the taxonomies includes a meaning that is rendered only upon translation of the word into

---

216  They combine the "methodological" and the "interpretative" nuance or logic. Note that 'nuance' and 'logic' are used interchangeably.

217  See Chapter I (A) "A Concept of Harm".

218  It could be considered incitement to discrimination perhaps.

219  Johnson, 'Swearing: The Last Taboos' (Blog: *Prospero*, 21 January 2015), available at: https://www.economist.com/blogs/prospero/2015/01/johnson-swearing.

the local language.[220] Chapter V presents an alternative taxonomy to overcome these limitations.

## Conclusion

This chapter presented the development of a legally-constructed, transactable property right in trademarks. It analysed morality and public order as a basis of state intervention to restrict trademark rights and presented linguistic variations in morality exclusions between countries. Humanistic terms such as "respect" and "honour" were unique to non-Western jurisdictions and suggest a broader, more consumer-focused prohibitory mandate. Express clauses protecting religious sensibilities were also found. These variations suggest that trademark law cannot be separated from cultural norms. The chapter also showed that the morality and public order distinction has been extensively explored in Western jurisprudence, yet it remains somewhat elusive. GCC trademark practitioners are not yet engaged in this intellectual exercise. Finally, the chapter critiqued current approaches to classifying objectionable signs. It introduced a concept of methodological and interpretative nuance in order to clarify distinct and consecutive logics that drive the examination of trademarks under the prohibition.

---

220  It would not replace logic 1. After translation, logic 1 would still need to be applied. Most often the meaning would be rendered by the literal meaning of the translated word.

# III. The trademark system of the Gulf Cooperation Council (GCC)

## Introduction

This chapter sets out the trademark system in the GCC. Part A explains the religious foundations of these countries in order to increase understanding of the GCC position on the registrability of trademarks that raise cultural and public moral concerns. Part B outlines each country's international obligations based on membership of international treaties. Part C discusses the new GCC Trademark Law, which is not yet implemented by all members. The chapter highlights the main challenges to this harmonisation. Part D briefly introduces two peculiarities of trademark regulation in Arab league countries: first, the contentious issue of trademark rights denied to firms linked to a boycotted country, and, second, the prohibition on product classes that violate public morals and religious teachings. Part E considers how a selection of trademarks accepted by EU and/or US examiners would likely be treated by GCC examiners.

## A. Legal system, Shari'a law

*Legal sources of Islamic law.* Islamic countries have both codified and non-codified sources of Islamic law. Codified sources have higher importance. They are: the *Qur'an*, the *Sunnah* (primary sources), and *ijma*.[221] Non-codified law comprises '*qiyas*' and '*ijtihad*'.[222] 'Qiyas' is the concept of strict logical reasoning by analogy and is used to resolve conflict among the three codified sources. Ijtihad' is a jurist's tool in Islamic law and jurisprudence that encourages independent thought and deliberation to resolve problems where the other sources of law are silent. These sources form the body of Islamic religious law known as Shari'a law – the law of the Qur'an and the religious law of Muslims.

---

221 Consensus on a point of law by authorized religious scholars after the death of the Prophet.
222 Khoury (n 125).

*Shari'a.* Shari'a' (Arabic: شريعة) means "the road to the watering place", or the "clear path of commandment" to be followed.[223] This is important in the context of legal certainty and evolving norms discussed in Chapter II. Western jurisdictions deal with general rules and apply them to specific instances. Shari'a in contrast does not expound general legal principles, "it rather deals with specific instances, or transactions, and propounds rules relating thereto.... general principles must be deduced by analogy."[224] While the text of the Qur'an cannot be changed or contradicted, critical reasoning through ijtihad allows interpretation to draw modern meaning. However, it is considered a prestigious task reserved for qualified religious scholars. Its relevance as a legal tool is said to have disappeared in the early tenth century.[225] 'Qiyas' remains a legal norm that judges can employ but its use is limited.

*Real property and intellectual property, (IP).* The Qur'an does not expressly address intellectual property protection but it recognises certain legal concepts that function as a legal basis for IP protection, particularly protection of trademarks.[226] These are: personal rights and autonomy (*Haqq*), the right to income/accumulate wealth *(Mal)* (but in the hierarchy of values, morality is higher),[227] real property rights (private ownership of property cf. absolute ownership which is to God), the right to acquire real property including acquiring new or unclaimed items, and loss of title due to non-use.

*Constitutions.* Shari'a law is enshrined in the constitution of the U.A.E by Article 7 of the U.A.E Constitution,[228] in the constitution of Qatar by Arti-

---

223  W. M. Ballantyne. Essays and Addresses on Arab Laws (Curzon Press 2000) 33.

224  ibid 34.

225  ibid 41. Although some reformist Muslim thinkers question the immutability of the text and seek a revival of ijtihad for modern society. See, for instance, Tariq Ramadan 'Radical Reform: Islamic Ethics and Liberation (OUP 2009).

226  Khoury (n 125), citing, Ida Madieha Azmi, Spyros M. Maniatis & Bankole Sodipo, Distinctive Signs and Early Markets: Europe, Africa, and Islam, in Perspectives on Intellectual Property.: The Prehistory and Development of Intellectual Property Systems Vol. 1, 123, 132 (Alison Firth ed., Sweet & Maxwell 1997).

227  Khoury (n 125) 77, citing, Syed Nawab Haidar Naqvi, Islam, Economics and Society 73 (Kegan Paul. Intl. 1994)

228  The Constitution of the UAE (1971). The Arabic version is the definitive legal text. Available at: https://wipolex.wipo.int/en/text/440262. Article 7: "Islam is the official religion of the UAE. The Islamic Shari'a is a main source of legislation in the UAE. The official language of the UAE is Arabic."

cle 1 of the Constitution of the State of Qatar,[229] and in the constitution of Saudi Arabia by Article 1 of its Basic Law of Governance.[230] However, levels of conservatism differ. This is perhaps hinted at in the wording of the opening articles of the Saudi Arabian and Qatari Constitutions; the former recognises Shari'a as all encompassing, almost one and the same ("the constitution *is…*"). The latter places Shari'a as "the *main* source…".

The GCC states have large expatriate populations and high immigration, notably the UAE and Qatar. Saudi Arabia has the highest proportion of national citizens with 67.3% Saudi nationals. Emiratis comprise only 11.5% of the UAE population, while 14.3% of Qatar's population is Qatari.[231]

*Saudi Arabia*. Arabic is the official language and Islam is the official religion. Citizens are Muslim. Sunni Islam is the dominant sect. The population is 31m in 2015.[232] Article 7 of the Constitution of Saudi Arabia establishes the primacy of Islamic law: "The authority of the regime is derived from the Holy Qur'an and the prophet's Sunnah which rule over this and all other state laws." The interests of the state and the relationship with citizens are made clear in Articles 10-12. It is the resolve and duty of the state to "strengthen the bonds which hold the family together and to preserve its Arab and Islamic values" (Article 10); the state seeks to avoid "dissension" (Article 11) and will prohibit things that may "**lead to** disunity, sedition and division" (Article 12). The right to property is recognised, how-

---

229  The Constitution of the State of Qatar (2004). English translation. The Arabic version is the definitive legal text. Available at: https://wipolex.wipo.int/en/legisl ation/details/9626. Article 1: "Qatar is an independent sovereign Arab State. Its religion is Islam and Shari'a law shall be a main source of its legislations. Its political system is democratic. The Arabic Language shall be its official language. The people of Qatar are a part of the Arab nation."

230  Basic Law of Governance (promulgated by the Royal Decree No. A/90 dated 27/08/1412H (March 1, 1992)). English translation. The Arabic version is the definitive legal text. Available at: https://wipolex.wipo.int/en/legislation/details/7 973. Article 1 establishes the Shari'a and the Sunnah as its 'constitution' although there is no formal constitution as such: "The kingdom of Saudi Arabia is a sovereign Arab Islamic state. Its religion is Islam, and its constitution is the Holy Qur'an and the prophet's (peace be upon him) Sunnah (traditions). Its language is the Arabic language, and its capital city is Riyadh."

231  31 March 2015 statistics, available at the Demographic and Economic Database, Gulf Labour Markets and Migration website.

232  31million in 2015 according to Gulf Migration, available at: http://gulfmigratio n.eu/glmm-database/demographic-and-economic-module/?search=1&cmct=Sau di+Arabia. CIA World Factbook 28.6million in 2016 https://www.cia.gov/library /publications/the-world-factbook/geos/sa.html.

ever it is not absolute and the state can expropriate property in the public interest.[233]

*UAE.* Both Abu Dhabi (the capital) and Dubai are commercial centres and the most populated of the seven emirates. The UAE population is 6 million as of July 2017.[234] Dubai has the largest population of 2.4 million.[235] The UAE has the seventh highest net migration rate in the world (12.36%). The majority of expatriates are Asians (75%). Westerners follow at 8%.[236] Arabic is the official language and Islam is the official religion (approx. 76% are Muslims).[237]

*Qatar.* English is commonly used as a second language, especially in business. Islam is the official religion, with 67.7% Muslims, 13.8% Christian, 13.8% Hindus. The population is 2.3m as at July 2017.[238] The words "morals" and "ethics" are expressly stated in the Constitution of Qatar: Part Two is dedicated to "The Guiding Principles of Society". Article 21 states "the family is the basis of the society. A Qatari family is founded on religion, **ethics**, and patriotism". "[H]igh **morals**" are one of the values upon which Qatari Society is said to be based (Article 18). Private property rights are recognised and limited: "Private property is inviolable; and no one shall be deprived of his property save by reason of public benefit and in the cases prescribed by the law."[239]

## B. *GCC IP Treaty Memberships*

The Gulf Cooperation Council (GCC) is an economic and political alliance between six countries in the Arabian Peninsula, all of which are autocracies: the United Arab Emirates (U.A.E.), Bahrain, Qatar, Saudi Arabia, Oman, and Kuwait. The GCC is "the Middle East's most important region-

---

233 Basic Law of Governance Article 1 (1992) Article 18. "The inviolability of private property shall be guaranteed by the state. Private property shall not be expropriated unless in the public interest, and the owner shall be fairly compensated".

234 Available at: https://www.cia.gov/library/publications/the-world-factbook/geos/qa.html. Although the United Nations puts it at 9.3million.

235 End 2015 data, Dubai Statistics Centre.

236 2017 data, available at: http://worldpopulationreview.com/countries/united-arab-emirates-population/.

237 See: https://www.cia.gov/library/publications/the-world-factbook/geos/ae.html.

238 See: https://www.cia.gov/library/publications/the-world-factbook/geos/qa.html

239 Article 17 Charter of Fundamental Rights of the European Union, available at: http://eur-lex.europa.eu/legal-content/EN/TXT/?uri=CELEX%3A12012P%2FTXT

al organisation."[240] Saudi Arabia is the dominant member.[241] All are first-to-register jurisdictions and there is no common law tort of "passing off". Each state has its own intellectual property laws and there are also unifying laws (the 1987 GCC Patent Law and the 2006 GCC Trademark Law).[242] They are contracting parties to the principal international IP-related multilateral treaties (see Table 1): **[1] WIPO-administered treaties:** the Berne Convention, Paris Convention,[243] Patent Cooperation Treaty. Only Bahrain and Oman are Madrid Union members (parties to the Madrid Protocol). None is a party to the Madrid Agreement;[244] **[2] The World Trade Organisation:**[245] as WTO members, they are bound by the **Agreement on Trade Related Aspects of Intellectual Property Rights** (TRIPS Agreement, 1994), which sets minimum standards for protection of intellectual property and must be transposed through legislation and/or case law. The GCC countries, with the exception of Bahrain,[246] are not parties to **The Nice Agreement.**[247] However, they apply the Nice Classification to categorise

---

240  Anoushiravan Ehteshami, 'GCC Foreign policy: From the Iran-Iraq War to the Arab Awakening' LSE Middle East Centre collected papers, Vol 1. April 2015, available at: http://eprints.lse.ac.uk/

241  ibid 13. Ehteshami refers to its "geographical domination"; Dar & Pesley, 2006, 'The Gulf Co-Operation Council: A Slow Path to Integration?' 24 World Eco. No.9, 1161.

242  Only the Patent Law is 'unitary'.

243  The Convention took effect in Qatar July 5, 2000; Saudi Arabia March 11, 2004; U.A.E. September 19, 1996; Kuwait December 2, 2014; Bahrain October 29, 1997; Oman July 14, 1999. See http://www.wipo.int/treaties/en/ip/paris/.

244  The Madrid-based International Trademarking System allows a bundle of national applications to ensue from a single international application. See http://www.wipo.int/export/sites/www/treaties/en/documents/pdf/madrid_marks.pdf.

245  Qatar acceded January 13, 1996; Saudi Arabia acceded December 11, 2005; Qatar acceded January 13, 1996; Bahrain acceded January 1, 1995; Kuwait acceded January 1, 1995; Oman acceded November 9, 2000 (WIPO). List of members available at: http://www.wipo.int/wipolex/en/other_treaties/parties.jsp?treaty_id=231&group_id=22.

246  Entry into force: December 15, 2005.

247  The Agreement was established in 1957 at the Nice Diplomatic Conference. It established an international classification of goods and services for the purposes of registering trademarks. It has been revised twice (1967 at Stockholm, and 1977 at Geneva) and amended once (1979). The 11th edition of the Agreement entered into force on January 1, 2017, available at: http://www.wipo.int/classifications/nice/en/preface.html.

items for national registration of marks.[248] Different editions of the Nice Classification are in use: the U.A.E. uses the 10th edition, Qatar uses the latest 11th edition,[249] Kuwait uses the 8th edition and Bahrain and Oman use the 10th edition.[250] The use of different editions may reduce the efficiency of filing in several jurisdictions. Saudi Arabia uses its own adapted version of Nice.[251] It contains the products permitted in Saudi applications. However, some items are included that would still certainly be rejected.[252] Only the specific terms in the list can be used in the specification filed, so applicants cannot circumvent an objection by amending the wording.

Table 1: Membership of multilateral agreements in the six jurisdictions.[253]

| Country | Madrid System | | Nice Agreement | Nice Edition | TRIPS | Paris Convention |
|---------|------------|------------|-----------------|--------------|-------|------------------|
| | MA 1891 | MP 1989 | | | | |
| UAE | No | No | No | 10th | Yes | Yes |
| Qatar | No | No | No | 11th (45 Classes) | Yes | Yes |
| Saudi Arabia | No | No | No | 10th | Yes | Yes |
| Bahrain | No | Yes – 2005 | Yes | 10th | Yes | Yes |
| Kuwait | No | No | No | 8th | Yes | Yes |
| Oman | No | Yes – 2007 | No | 10th | Yes | Yes |

---

248 Perhaps this ensures they have autonomy with respect to what classification categories they recognise, although Article 2 of the Nice Agreement permits signatories to exclude certain classification categories.

249 World Trademark Review Issue 67, 11.

250 http://www.sabaip.com/en/Resources/IP-Tables/General-Information-on-Nice-Cl assification-in-the-MENA

251 التصنيف الدولي للسلع والخدمات (اتفاقية نيس) (International Classification of Goods and Services (Nice Agreement), at the Trademark Office website.

252 For example, dating services in Class 45, love dolls in Class 10, gambling in Class 41, bar services in Class 43, pork and ham in Class 29, ham glaze in Class 30, Christmas trees in Class 31.

253 Compiled using WIPO statistics. Bahrain shows most participation. Price attributes this to the Free Trade Agreements Bahrain has signed with the US. See Price (n 129).

## C. Harmonisation

The GCC Trademark Law was enacted by the GCC Supreme Council in December 2006 and approved in 2014.[254] It was the culmination of a twenty-year effort.[255] It sets out unifying provisions and standards for registration and enforcement of trademarks across the six GCC states. It should be noted that it is a harmonisation effort, not a unitary law. This means there is no unitary registration or enforcement system and trademarks still need to be registered on a national basis at each national trademark office. A company marketing products or services in all six states must file six separate applications at the six national receiving offices. There are slight differences in the procedural aspects of the national laws. As discussed, Saudi Arabia uses the trademark law in conjunction with the Shari'a law. The law has been ratified by all GCC states[256]but is not effective until implementation regulations are issued. To date, Kuwait, Bahrain, Saudi Arabia and Oman have issued implementing regulations,[257] but it is not clear how far they have gone in applying the new provisions. Excluded Nice classification categories are enumerated in implementing regulations.

*Public order and morality provisions.* The morality and public order exclusions in the new GCC Trademark Law are an amalgamation of the national provisions. Article 3 prohibits registration as a trade mark or an element thereof:-[258]

(2) Any mark breaching the public morals or violating the public order.
(4) Logos of the Red Crescent or Red Cross and such other similar symbols and the marks being an imitation thereof.
(5) Marks that are identical or similar to symbols having a purely religious character

*Obstacles to successful harmonisation.* Cultural divergence between GCC countries creates inconsistency in outcomes. An international brand operating in several GCC countries may need to adapt the brand not just for the MENA or GCC region as a whole, but potentially for individual countries, as shown by brands such as NKD PIZZA and Dr ORGANIC (Figure 2). Following rejections in the GCC, NAKED/NAKED PIZZA took the

---

254  GCC Trademark Law (n 45).
255  Price (n 129), 88.
256  Implementing Regulations by Oman's authorities are pending.
257  The GCC Trade Mark Law automatically comes into force six months after the Implementing Regulations have been published
258  See (n 45) Article 3 (2)(4)(5).

opportunity to rebrand globally to NKD. Dr Organic sought to register its logo containing the globally-recognizable pharmacy cross. It was rejected in Saudi Arabia but proceeded without objection in the UAE.[259] The Egyptian application was also rejected. Advertising campaigns may also need to be adapted. In Unilever's local campaign for its AXE deodorant, the company sought alternative ways to convey the sexual attraction message (Figure 3). Unilever's 2016 campaign "Axe Find Your Magic" and it's 2017 UK/US campaign "Is It OK for Guys", present interesting issues.[260] The campaign is a shift away from gender stereotypes. Such messages challenging traditional concepts of masculinity that prevail elsewhere, could be met with objection in MENA/GCC.

Figure 2: Examples of adapted marks.

| Brand | Trademark | |
|---|---|---|
| NAKED PIZZA | Global | UAE |
| | NAKED PIZZA® | ▾nkdpizza |
| DR. ORGANIC | Dubai | Saudi Arabia |
| | dr.organic® | dr.organic® |

---

259  Survey responses.
260  Is it Ok for Guys: https://www.youtube.com/watch?v=0WySfa7x5q0; Find Your Magic: https://www.youtube.com/watch?v=OOftlcikaRQ

Figure 3: Examples of adapted advertising campaigns.

| | Original marketing | Middle East marketing |
|---|---|---|
| UNILEVER's AXE deodorant |  |  |
| GIVENCHY perfume |  Original Western advertisement "Ange or demon" | 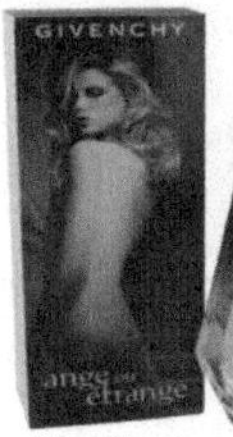 Saudi adaptation "Ange ou étrange" |

The UAE is a federation of seven Emirates. Decisions on trademark applications in Dubai often follow the standard of the most conservative Emirate, which is Abu Dhabi. Applying this logic at the GCC level, the lowest common denominator is the most conservative (Saudi Arabia). Thus, it remains to be seen whether there will be one (ultra-conservative) standard or a mixture of contradictory results that cannot easily be reconciled. Decorations for Christmas trees in Class 28 have been rejected in Saudi Arabia and accepted in the UAE. Applicants consistently choose to abandon the application and adopt a different mark, rather than go through appeal proceedings.[261]

Article 51 of the Act appears to place the GCC Trade Cooperation Committee (TCC) in a 'European Court of Justice' type of role, whereby it interprets the law for the individual national courts. However, there is no

---

261 This statement is true of the UAE, based on survey responses. It is not verified for other GCC jurisdictions.

central court to facilitate consistent interpretation by the national courts and no further details on how questions will be brought to the TCC.

A particularity is that only two of the GCC countries belong to the Madrid system. These countries can still reject an International Registration on morality grounds. However, undertakings using Madrid in Arab countries and also designating Israel, risked being rejected under the secondary level of the Arab League boycott of Israel.[262] Undertakings are advised to designate Arab countries under the Madrid system and file nationally in Israel.[263]

The case-law review conducted for this paper signals a problem of inconsistent results in the GCC. But note that commentators point to the same problem in other jurisdictions.[264]

## D. Boycotts and banned goods

### 1. Boycott ("prohibition to deal") clause

The Arab League[265] has implemented and maintained a trade boycott of Israel since 1945.[266] Notwithstanding its non-binding nature, the boycott is

---

262 See Part D, "Boycotts and Banned Goods".

263 No instances of this have been noted other than in Egypt and Syria, and this may not be the current practice given that the GCC is no longer enforcing the secondary level of the Boycott.

264 See Chapter I (C).

265 Twenty two Middle Eastern and African members countries, of which twelve are also WTO members.

266 The boycott began in 1945 and was formalised in 1948 upon Israel's proclamation of 'independence'. There are three levels: The primary boycott applies at the citizen level, prohibiting citizens of Arab League members from "buying from, selling to, or entering into a business contract with either the Israeli government or an Israeli citizen"; bits citizens of an Arab League member from buying, selling to, or entering into a business contract with either the Israeli government or an Israeli citizen" The secondary boycott blacklists businesses that have commercial ties with Israel. The tertiary boycott "prohibits an Arab League member and its nationals from doing business with a company that deals with companies that have been blacklisted by the Arab League". Not all countries enforce the boycott but details on this are vague. See the Congressional Research Service (CRS) report on the Arab League Boycott of Israel (August 2017) available at: https://fas.org/sgp/crs/mideast/RL33961.pdf.

reflected in the national trademark regulations of some GCC countries,[267] as a "prohibition-to-deal" clause, [268] [269] This clause is also present in the GCC Trade Mark Law. Article 3(10) prohibits from registration, "marks owned by natural or legal persons with whom it is prohibited to deal as per a resolution passed by the Competent Authority in this regard". The situation raises a 'national treatment' issue.[270] Survey responses did not indicate cases of rejected or cancelled trademarks arising on this ground.

Some Arab League members no longer participate in all levels of the boycott.[271] The UAE, Qatar, and Saudi Arabia are among countries that enforced the secondary boycott which affects companies doing business with Israel. However, accession to the WTO led to a softening of this stance and in 1994, the GCC announced it would only enforce the primary boycott. The previous provision (TML 1992A, article 24) in the UAE law that gave the Israeli Boycott Office the power to order the Ministry to cancel the registration of a trademark is absent from the GCC Trademark Law.

## 2. Banned items: products and services that cannot be trademarked

Even if a trademark has no immoral meaning (i.e. it is not objectionable on its face, by innuendo, in the context of the goods, or in the context of the criminal message promoted), the goods or services to which it is to be affixed or applied may themselves be deemed immoral or harmful. It is possible to identify two sub-categories of such goods/services: items that

---

267  Including the UAE (Article 24 TML 1992A, TMR 1993 Article 34) and Saudi Arabia (Article 2(11)).

268  Law No. 9 of 2002 on Trademarks, Trade Names, Geographical Indications and Industrial Designs.

269  Research for this paper found no express clause in the trademark laws of Bahrain, Oman, or Qatar but it may be enacted elsewhere. It is conceivable that, in the absence of a specific clause in the trademark laws, the policy could continue to live under the 'public order' provision, given the overwhelming public sentiment among the populations in these countries.

270  "National treatment" is an important rule laid down in Article 2 of the Paris Convention that nationals of each member state enjoy, in the other member states, the same intellectual property protections granted to nationals of those member states. This creates a delicate situation if a country is a contracting party to the Paris convention and trade or diplomatic relations have been severed as part of political solidarity.

271  See Congressional Research Service (CRS) report on the Arab League Boycott of Israel (August 2017), available at: https://fas.org/sgp/crs/mideast/RL33961.pdf.

are illegal under the laws of a country and items that are legal but nevertheless harmful and restricted.

In the GCC, trademarks cannot be registered for products and services that are against religious teachings. These include: alcoholic beverages, pork products, gambling services, escort services, and discos. Some of these goods and services are entirely illegal, such as abortion services, casinos, gambling and escort services. Others like pork, alcohol and discos fall between what is legal and what is illegal. Under Shari'a law and for Muslims, they are not permitted. But due to the large expatriate population the goods and services are available although closely regulated.[272]

*Borderline goods.* Some less-obvious unregistrable products are:

– **Non-Islamic religious charities, services and products**
   These items could raise issues if they involve symbols or are considered symbolic, and be rejected for being "identical or similar to symbols having a purely religious character".[273] If no symbols are involved, the application may be accepted. However, it has a better chance if the filing is worded more generally, such as, "charitable services", thereby avoiding religious specification.[274] Saudi law is broader than the Qatari and UAE law and would reject on the basis of "violating religion".[275]

– **Sex toys or similar goods**
   These are likely to be rejected under 'public morals' and 'public order' provisions.[276] [277] Other products like lubricating gels, etc., are likely to be accepted as long as they are not explicitly outlined in the specification. Applicants should use general terms to minimise potential issues.[278]

*Illegal goods.* Upstream moral bars are applied by the GCC by prohibiting registration for illegal products and services. This is a lawful limitation of rights by the state, recognised globally. As Dean J in *New South Wales Dairy Corp* articulated: "Registration of a trade mark does not ordinarily consti-

---

272  Survey responses. This is true of the UAE and Qatar, not Saudi Arabia.
273  Article 3(5) of the UAE Trademark Law.
274  Survey responses.
275  Article 2(b): any expression or sign or drawing violating religion, which is identical or similar to a symbol of religious nature."
276  Article 3(2) of the UAE Trade Mark Law, Article 3(2) of GCC Trade Mark Law, Article 2(c) Saudi Trade Mark Law, Article 8(2) Qatar Trade Mark Law.
277  Survey responses. See also: http://www.emaratalyoum.com/local-section/other/2 011-04-23-1.384040.
278  Survey responses.

tute a license for what would otherwise be unlawful conduct." [279] The U.K. Trade Marks Act 1993(2) excludes items that are "prohibited by law". The U.S. and Canada[280] apply an 'unlawful use' doctrine to prohibit trademarks for illegal goods and services. If the item is illegal under federal law, the associated trademark cannot be registered on the Principal Register as it will be considered federally illegal and "scandalous" under section 2(a).[281]

*Harmful goods: appropriation of IP rights and Article 7 Paris Convention.*[282] Downstream public health restrictions are affecting trademark rights in some Western countries. Post-registration brand restrictions are applied to restrict the *use* of registered trademarks on products like tobacco.

## E. Prospects for registrability in the GCC

The Constitutional language of GCC states indicates a low threshold for harm-based intervention.[283] The governments take on a dominating role as protector of the fabric of society, family structure, ethics and religious values. Qatar's constitution states: "The family is the basis of society.... founded on religion, ethics and patriotism. The law shall regulate adequate means to protect the family, support its structure, strengthen its ties, and protect maternity, childhood and old age".[284] The State vows to protect the young from "corruption [and] exploitation."[285] Saudi Arabia's Basic Law of Governance recognises the family as the "nucleus" of Saudi society.[286] The State assumes responsibility for "strengthen[ing] family bonds" and "main-

---

279  *New South Wales Dairy Corp v Murray Goulburn Co-op Co Ltd [1991] R.P.C.*

280  *McCabe v. Yamamoto & Co. (America) Inc. (1989), 23 C.P.R. (3d) 498 (F.C.T.D.).*

281  Twenty eight U.S. states have legalized cannabis. This means it can be entered into state registers.. To circumvent federal restriction, cannabis companies are trademarking not the cannabis products/supply service but ancillary products and services e.g. t-shirts, hats etc. This is a way of creating an exclusionary right for the cannabis service without having it, if they can build up a brand, others will be discouraged from copying and selling cannabis under the brand.

282  Bilateral investment treaties. Qatar has bilateral investment treaties (BITs) with Finland, Russia, Turkey, and India. No BITS are recorded for Saudi Arabia or the U.A.E according to WIPO's records.

283  See Chapter II.

284  Article 21 Constitution of Qatar.

285  Article 22 Constitution of Qatar.

286  Article 9 Basic Law of Governance Royal Order No. (A/91), 27 Sha'ban 1412H – 1 March 1992.

tain[ing] its Arab and Islamic values".[287] The State "shall protect the Islamic creed, apply its Shari'ah, enjoin the good and prohibit evil, and carry out the duty of calling to God." [288]Members should "maintain solidarity and avoid dissension." [289]The State shall "prevent whatever leads to disunity, sedition and division." [290]

*Deriving meaning from words and symbols.* Batey[291] discusses dimensions of meaning in texts. Two different kinds of associations give meaning to text: denotation and connotation. These seem to be species of the genus 'meaning'. Denotation is the literal meaning of a word/language. Connotation is fluid, subjective, symbolic: "[I]t includes the feelings and emotions a word evokes in people and the sociocultural and personal associations that arise from that person's race, class, gender, religion". According to Batey, consumers employ both denotation and connotation to draw meaning from words. But *association* in the mind of the consumer precedes meaning. Thus, it is necessary to identify the associations evoked before the meaning can be understood. Applying Batey's logic to symbols rather than words, a pertinent example for this paper would be the Christian cross. It *denotes* the instrument by which Jesus was crucified. The *connotation* to Muslims is an allegory of persecution, the Crusades of the medieval period. Thus, Batey's thesis seems relevant for understanding trademark registration decisions.

In the context of cultural norms in Gulf societies, and the ways through which meaning is derived from texts, it is possible to speculate whether or not a given trademark would be accepted onto the register. The following is a sample of EU/ US-registered trademarks or unregistered brands. It presents the evaluations that might be expected in the GCC. It aims to provide additional insight and clarity on the thinking in the GCC. The observations are based on the opinions of local law firms.[292] [293]

---

287  Article 10 Basic Law of Governance Royal Order No. (A/91), 27 Sha'ban 1412H – 1 March 1992

288  Article 23.

289  Article 11 Basic Law of Governance Royal Order No. (A/91), 27 Sha'ban 1412H – 1 March 1992.

290  Article 12 Basic Law of Governance Royal Order No. (A/91), 27 Sha'ban 1412H – 1 March 1992.

291  Mark Batey, *Brand Meaning* (Routledge 2008) Ch 4.

292  Survey responses.

293  There is consensus in most cases among UAE, Qatar and Saudi attorneys. Where there is variation an overall determination is offered to reconcile the contrasting views.

| Mark | Religious connotation/blasphemy |
|---|---|
| **athé** <br> vanessabruno | Athé is the French word for "athiest". Unless the examiner is unaware of the meaning, it is highly likely to be rejected for "*violating religion*" in Saudi Arabia, and on policy grounds in the UAE and Qatar. |
| | Breath of God. <br> As above. |
| **OMG** | This trademark "OMG" is analogous to "TGI [Friday's]". It may meet with objection if the acronym is spelled out in the application "oh my God", but not if it is applied as the acronym. The odds are fairly even. |
| iCREATE | This mark is more likely than not to be accepted if the goods and services are such that it does not conjure the concept of God's creation. It is not inconceivable that a conservative examiner would conjure this meaning. In that case, the removal of "i" could help. |
| | **Sexual connotation** |
| KISS by Rihanna | Opinion was divided on whether this mark would proceed to registration in the GCC. 'Kiss' is problematic in that it can be ascribed an innocent meaning (kiss in the form of a greeting), or a more 'haram' meaning (pre- or extra-marital kiss), or the most explicit meaning which is the Arabic meaning of female genitalia. Generally, it is likely to escape the translated connotation in most cases but there is no guarantee. "Kisses" was rejected in Saudi Arabia for Class 30 goods in 2017 in the first instance and on appeal. Nevertheless, many "kiss" formative marks have been successfully registered in the UAE (AQUA KISS cl 3 for Victoria's Secret Stores Brand Management, Inc. KISS-KISS cl 14 for FMTM Distribution Ltd. POCKETKISS cl 3 for Bath & Body Works Brand Management, Inc.), Qatar, and Saudi Arabia (BIG KISS, KISS, KISS RESIST...) in different Classes. |
| BETTER THAN SEX MASCARA | This trademark is highly likely to be rejected under the public morals and public order prohibition. The applicant would likely need to remove the offending term "sex", or render it suggestive "Better than...? Mascara". |

| | |
|---|---|
| **MISS** ◊ **BIKINI**'<br><br>B<sup>kini</sup>sland | Opinion was divided on whether these two trademarks "Miss Bikini" and "Bikini Island" would proceed to registration in the GCC. Two respondents opined that both the word 'bikini' and the 'bikini devices' (bikini briefs; woman in a bikini) would raise objection. One respondent distinguished "Bikini Island" as more susceptible to rejection. In relation to "Miss Bikini", registrability may depend on whether the examiner would be swayed by the applicant's description in the specification of a "heart-shaped logo which is split into three parts" rather than "bikini briefs". |
| TANTRIC CONDOMS<br><br>SMART GIRL CONDOMS<br><br>OMG CONDOMS | Opinion was divided on whether these three trademarks for condoms would proceed to registration in the GCC. As discussed in Part **D.2.** of this Chapter, condoms would not normally face objection. Indeed, Durex is a registered trademark in the UAE, Qatar and Saudi. But these three trademarks carry additional connotations. Some respondents expected the marks to be rejected on morality and public order grounds. The connotation of "tantric" sex was highlighted by one respondent. Another respondent recommended removing the word "condom" entirely as a way of minimising objection and also broadening protection. Certainly, tantric alone may still be rejected. |
| | **Sedition?...** |
| ANARCHY (deodorant spray)<br><br>ANARCHY REIGNS (PlayStation game) | Opinion was divided on whether these two trademarks would proceed to registration in the GCC. Some responses indicated they may fall foul of the public order provision though not necessarily. Other responses fell on either side; on the one side, it was suggested that the mark would be rejected, especially following the 'Arab Spring'. The fact that "Anarchy Reigns" was related to a PlayStation game would not matter. On the other side, it was asserted that these would proceed to registration. |
| | **Taboo** |
| TOMBOYX | This trademark divided opinion. Some respondents considered that such a mark would be rejected on morality and public order grounds. The idea of non-traditional gender roles could be problematic. Indeed, any hint of cross-dressing or homosexuality is taboo and sits uncomfortably with Islamic teachings. However, it is possible that the examiner would not pick up on the meaning if the applicant stated in the application that it is a made-up word (by virtue of the 'X'). |
| GIRLFRIEND | This is a borderline case in the sense that it would likely be rejected as the concept of a girlfriend or boyfriend is not recognised in Islam, however, it could succeed on appeal. |

*Conclusion*

This chapter examined the legal system and cultural norms of the GGC Region. It found that the constitutional language provides a window into the treatment of inappropriate trademarks at the practitioner level. Because Islamic law is enshrined in the constitutions of GCC states, the desire to shield citizens from influences that are not conducive to the public good is a predominant factor. The chapter revealed high expatriate populations in these countries, which has implications for the "relevant public" as a legal standard for assessing registrability and infringement in the Region. Finally, a small selection of ostensibly innocuous signs was presented to local practitioners to test the prognosis for successful registration in the GCC. Responses showed a level of uncertainty with regard to how examiners would perceive the signs. Despite this uncertainty, responses affirmed the fact that fading taboos in the West remain intact in Gulf societies. Even mildly risqué marks may be refused. An important insight for brand owners is that some concepts are simply not recognised in Islamic cultures. Signs or advertising suggestive of androgyny or cross-dressing, for instance, are unlikely to proceed to registration in the GCC. Similarly, signs suggestive of sex or pre-marital relationships (boyfriend, girlfriend) are also at risk of refusal. Notwithstanding this fact, applicants can improve prospects by drafting the description in the specification in general terms. In the event of insurmountable objections, companies can seize new opportunities such as global rebranding, as in the case of NAKED/NKD.

# IV. Dominant rationales in applying moral exclusions

## Introduction

This chapter explores the reasons for efforts to prohibit the registration of immoral marks in the GCC, with jurisdictional contrast from Europe/UK and the U.S. In the absence of precedents and published reasoning in the GCC, there is some conjecture involved. The insights are drawn from opinions of local law firms, as well as independent analysis based on the literature canvassed in previous chapters of this paper. Part A discusses the rationales. Part B introduces a couple of interesting aspects of GCC practice in assessing trademarks.

## A. Rationales

A survey conducted of five law firms in the UAE, Saudi Arabia and Qatar suggests that four main reasons (1-4) underlie examiner objections to offensive marks in these countries.[294]

1. *Concern that the public would be offended by the mark*
2. *Examiner directly applying the law without further thought*
3. *A deeper concern about the power of a mark to erode the morals of society*
4. *The State should not be seen to endorse such marks*
5. *The State should not spend its time or financial resources to support marks that are contrary to the values of society*[295]

---

294 With respect to Saudi Arabia, reasons1 and 2 were highlighted. UAE respondents considered reasons 1, 2, 3 and 4 to be the most common. Qatari counsel highlight reason 3.At least two firms confirmed each of the reasons 1-4. **Disclaimer**: The insights are to be considered in light of three factors [1] they are based on subjective opinions of trademark attorneys and not the examiners or Trade Mark Office officials; [2] they are derived from a small sample size; [3] surveys were completed remotely and it is assumed that respondents understood the rationales and the differences between them. Further research should test these preliminary observations. It should also be noted that respondents were asked to select from five rationales, which constituted a closed list.

295 Reason "5" - that the state's resources should not be wasted on such marks" - was not expressly confirmed by any respondents.

## 1. Concern that the public would be offended by the mark

This rationale concerns the *threshold* for public shock and offense. There are two elements to this threshold: (1) the intensity of the sense of affront, and (2) the breadth of its impact (proportion of the public affected). Intensity has been discussed elsewhere in this paper.[296] Regarding breadth, the 'relevant public' is considered. If moral principles function as a bar to trademark protection, the question is whose principles matter and how many people need to share them in order to activate the prohibition.

The question of how a mark that offends a group of people will be treated is pertinent to the GCC context, particularly the main commercial and cultural cities of Dubai, Abu Dhabi, and Doha. Since Emirati and Qatari nationals are minorities in their countries, if examiners applied the EU/UK approach, they may consider a mark that offends only Emiratis or Qataris insufficient to trigger the prohibition. However, examiners in the GCC do not adopt this nuanced approach.[297] If the examiner believes the mark will offend even a limited group, that will likely be sufficient for a rejection.[298] Hence, the GCC seems to diverge with respect to both elements; the threshold is lower and an objection will probably be raised if there is a hint that offence could be caused to a small group/small percentage of the population. It may even be enough that the examiner alone is offended or knows people who would be.[299] This stands in contrast to European/UK and US guidance for examiners/registrars who must set aside their personal opinions if it goes against an existing generally accepted moral code.[300]

It is not possible to say unequivocally whether examiners are as equally attuned to the sensibilities of other religions. The UAE, Qatar and Saudi Arabia are home to large populations of workers. The latter two groups come from countries like the Philippines, India, Nepal and Sri Lanka

---

296 See Chapter I.

297 The situation is potentially more complicated than this given that many of the non-nationals will also be Muslims from other Arab countries, South Asia etc. Thus, the Muslim population is considered to be a majority in these three states (very different from the Western contingents: 2.7% in the UK and 3.75% in the US - http://islamicweb.com). Despite this, whether or not offence is taken might still differ between Muslim groups: consider for example, an English-speaking Saudi Muslim, a non-English-speaking Nepalese migrant worker, a conservative Qatari Muslim and a Muslim from a secular country like Lebanon.

298 Survey responses.

299 Survey responses.

300 See, for instance, Richard Arnold QC, (n 191) at [37], citing Sir Nicolas Brown-Wilkinson V-C in case *Stephens v Avery [1988]*.

where Hinduism, Buddhism, Christian (Roman Catholicism), are dominant religions. In Saudi Arabia, since there is no official recognition of other religions, it is not clear how strictly trademarks that offend Buddhism, Hinduism would be treated. In the GCC, an application for BUDDHA BEER was rejected on morality grounds due to the reference to Buddha.[301]

If the Trade Mark Office is concerned with public offence, the possibility of changing attitudes among the public is relevant. There are differing views on whether there has been much change over the years in these Islamic countries. Some suggest a degree of change (notably UAE and Qatar),[302] however there is no corresponding change in the approach of trademark practitioners dealing with the fundamental morality, cultural and religious questions. In fact, in the UAE at least, examiners are being more cautious in accepting trademarks due to the increasing role of social media in publishing information. [303]

## 2. Direct application of the law

All respondents cited this rationale.[304] It relates to the black and white approach taken by trademark officials in the GCC, notwithstanding that examiners have complete discretion to interpret the morality of marks.

While this rationale governs most decisions in the GCC, it does not in the US, Europe or other common law jurisdictions. There are a few reasons for this. The UAE, Qatar and Saudi Arabia's laws and legal institutions are built on the civil law system, specifically French civil law (Napoleonic code) inherited from Egypt.[305] [306] [307] There is no system of binding precedent in civil law systems. Sharia, as well, lacks a binding precedent system.[308] As such, decisions appear as short citations of the relevant legal

---

301  See Chapter V. It is not known whether the nature of the goods was at issue.
302  Survey responses.
303  Survey responses.
304  Survey responses.
305  See http://www.tamimi.com/en/magazine/law-update/section-6/september-2/the
     -court-structure-in-qatar.html.
306  Hansen (n 12), xxvii.
307  Saudi Arabia's trademark law of 1939 (promulgated by High Order No. 8762, of
     September 12, 1939) was based on The Egyptian Trademark Law of July 9 1939.
     Habachy, S. (n.d.). Protection of Trademarks and Patent Rights in the Middle
     East History, Geography and Economics.
308  Khoury (n 125) 197.

provision. The fact that the legal profession in these countries is very young may also smother the kind of judicial interest in testing the boundaries of the law that is common in Western (common law) jurisdictions.[309]

Another reason is that the GCC countries do not have freedom of expression guarantees. Countries that do, are more likely to develop tests and guidelines that allow them to conduct a balancing exercise of the competing interests. EU and UK IP offices, in cases including MECHANICAL APARTHEID and JESUS, often invoke the applicant's right to commercial speech under Article 10 of the ECHR and explain the limits on state interference with it.[310] The test applied in European jurisprudence is that the interference has to be justifiable ("prescribed by law and necessary in a democratic society"). Free speech rights dominated THE SLANTS case. Thus, having such guarantees lends itself to a more nuanced approach.

Hansen notes that the GCC takes a literal and strict approach to trademarks and goods/services that are contrary to Islamic principles.[311] This means that the more nuanced aspects of Anglo-American case law are not present in trademark jurisprudence in the GCC. Trademark officials do not generally take into account the fact that a word is a parody.[312] In contrast, the UK/EU and the U.S. give more leeway to parody and puns, in keeping with freedom of expression. Nor do decision-makers in the GCC always consider the positive intentions of an applicant. Some decisions suggest there is allowance for signs with an innocent connotation. Other decisions appear to reject this pleading. See discussion under Part B of this chapter.

The more black and white position of the GCC countries may also be partly due to the lack of any formal examination guidelines for examiners in the UAE, Saudi Arabia or Qatar.[313] or any regular formal training carried out for the examiners. Without clear standards for assessing whether a mark is immoral, violates public order, or is of religious nature, it is left entirely to the discretion of the examiners.[314]

---

309 Hansen (n 12) xxix, with regard to the UAE legal profession observes that "the professions appear not to participate in any kind of disinterested activism for reform of laws and procedures".
310 Mechanical Apartheid R 2804/2014-5; JESUS (Basic Trademark n 9).
311 Hansen (n 12) 87. Although Hansen speaks of the UAE, the comment is applicable to the GCC as a whole, since the UAE is the most relaxed of the countries.
312 ibid.
313 One respondent indicates there may be some "standards" available from the Ministry of Commerce.
314 Survey responses.

In conclusion, the nuanced and publicised judicial reasoning of the common law systems and supranational law system of the EU (including civil law member states) lends itself to the development of sophisticated legal tests. The impact of Shari'a law in the GCC has created a more literal approach to regulation. Decisions normally just cite the legal provision. On the one hand this benefits applicants if decisions can be easily anticipated. However, when there is little balancing of interests traders might lose out to the public interest more than they would elsewhere.

### 3. A deeper concern about the power of a mark to erode the morals of society

In the Chapter III analysis, it was seen that the constitutions of the GCC states convey a paternal concern towards protecting society from decay. Trademarks rejected on morality grounds cannot be used in the GCC. This signifies a clear-cut approach to preventing immoral trademarks from flowing into society. Penalties for use of rejected marks are a fine and imprisonment.[315] U.S case law has expressly mentioned the notion of "*injury*".[316]

*Surprising rejections.* Some decisions to refuse to register a trademark can be unexpectedly strict. As discussed in Chapter III, the GCC states apply Shari'a in prohibiting certain Nice Classes and some products and services within allowed Classes. Trademarks for alcoholic related goods and services are proscribed under Shari'a law. Each country regulates its own trademark. Saudi Arabia differs from its neighbours in a few ways. As the most conservative state, it has a higher sensitivity to immoral marks compared to its neighbours. Another difference is that it is common for Shari'a principles to be applied by Saudi courts hearing appeals. If a mark is rejected, the applicant has 60 days to file an appeal with the Trade Mark Office. If the Trade Mark Office dismisses the appeal, the applicant has another 60 days to file an appeal with the Administrative Court in Riyadh. Decisions of the Administrative Court can be appealed to the Administrative Court of Appeals.[317] However, appeals are not common as applicants consistently

---

315  UAE Trademark Law: a fine of up to AED10,000 (equivalent to about USD $2,800) and/or up to one year in prison.

316  Oswald (n 151).

317  Survey responses.

choose to abandon the application and adopt a different mark, rather than go through appeal proceedings.[318]

The Shari'a principles most often cited by the courts are: (1) there should be neither harming nor reciprocating harm, (2) deception and anything that may mislead the people is forbidden, (3) damage and any excuse for corruption should be avoided. Saudi courts have applied the "no harm" principle ((1)), to reject registration of tobacco products, reasoning that because tobacco is harmful to one's health, it is forbidden. This upstream interference with trademark rights for public health reasons can be compared with the downstream brand restrictions by countries like the UK and Australia with Plain Packaging legislation.[319] If efforts to block registration of tobacco products were successful, it could encourage challenge under Article 7 of the Paris Convention since the sale and distribution of tobacco products are permitted. However, the courts have also cited fatwas (religious legal opinion)[320] declaring tobacco to be forbidden. Notwithstanding the preceding, the Saudi Trade Mark Office routinely registers trademarks for tobacco products as do the Trade Mark Offices of Qatari and the UAE.

## 4. The government should not provide official sanction to offensive marks

Commentators citing this reason include Wasserman,[321] Kelber,[322] and Oswald.[323] Kelber says federally registered marks carry "implied approval" of the government. Wasserman makes a strong argument that federal registration of pornographic trademarks perpetuates harmful discourse and subordination: "registration of these trademarks both amounts to a governmen-

---

318 Survey responses.

319 The UK introduced Plain Packaging legislation in 2017, Australia did so in 2012.

320 Fatwas are issuable in Saudi Arabia by qualified persons, these being approved religious scholars associated with the Council of Senior Ulema (per Royal Decree in August 2010, issued by the late King Abdullah (predecessor to current King Salman)). Ansary, D. A. F. (2008). A Brief Overview of the Saudi Arabian Legal System, 12. Available at: http://www.nyulawglobal.org/globalex/saudi_ara bia.htm

321 Wasserman (n 22) 6.

322 Bruce C. Kelber, 'Scalping the Redskins: Can Trademark Law Start Athletic Teams Bearing Native American Nicknames and Images on the Road to Racial Reform?' (1994) 17 Hamline L.Rev. 533, 560-61.

323 Oswald (n 151).

tal sanction of the goods and/or services the trademark represents, and works to undermine the nation's normative commitment to equality by assisting those who profit from sexual and racial subordination".[324] If courts/public bodies hold power to change societal prejudices, the correct application of morals bars is all the more important. If that power exists, then arguably the decisions of trademark officials should prioritise public policy goals over other interests. There are perhaps two subtle aspects to this rationale (rationale 4); it concerns: [1] the proper role of public bodies, and [2] the power that a particular judicial stance can have on moral and social norms. In defamation law, the courts have to consider the moral views of the time to understand if a particular imputation would lower someone's reputation and esteem. As noted earlier, judges in the common law tradition interpret and apply the law, and increasingly in a human-centric way to be consistent with the ECHR. Lo argues that the law has "limited effectiveness....to change societal prejudices" so individual needs should prevail.[325] This is not persuasive. Even if social prejudices trail behind the law, it is important for the law to take the authoritative stance and send the message. Arguably the law can provide gentle coercion to principles held by the public and thus normalise harmful attitudes. But, UK courts have urged an almost impossible balancing act: in the *Hallelujah* trademark case, Mr. Myall articulated that a Registrar "must not remain isolated from the day-to-day world, frozen in an outmoded set of moral principles, he must equally not presume to set the standard. He must certainly not act as a censor or arbiter of morals, nor yet as a trendsetter."[326]

However, several cases have rejected the notion that trademark registration constitutes government approval of a mark (and the point of view it expresses). In *Falcon Sporting Goods AG v. FIIP*, the Swiss Federal Board of Appeal for Intellectual Property Rights (Board of Appeal) overturned a revocation by the Swiss Federal Institute of Intellectual Property (FIIP) of *BIN LADIN* and allowed registration on the basis that it does not amount to endorsement of the September 11th terrorist attacks by Switzerland.[327] In UK design case, *Masterman's Design*, Aldous J stated that Registrars' deci-

---

324 Wasserman (n 22) 6, citing Gail Dines et al. "Pornography: The Production and Consumption of Inequality 20 (1998).

325 Available at: www.austlii.edu.au/au/journals/PolemicUSyd/2004/1.pdf.

326 *Hallelujah Trade Mark* [1976] RPC 605 (UK)

327 But note dissent from a minority of the Appeal Board. Falcon Sporting Goods AG v. FIIP, Case MA-RS 1/2. INTA Bulletin January 15, 2005, Vol 60, No. 2, available at: www.inta.org/INTABulletin/Pages/BINLADINTrademarkUpheld.aspx

sions are judicial not administrative.[328] In *Matal v. TAM*,[329] Justice Alito quipped "[i]f the federal registration of a trademark makes the mark government speech, the Federal Government is babbling prodigiously and incoherently". In *In re Old Glory Condom Corp.*,[330] the T.T.A.B. remarked that "the act of registration is not a government imprimatur". In *FCUK*,[331] Richard Arnold QC cited Aldous J's decision in *Masterman's Design*,[332] in which he dismissed the notion that the act of registration signals endorsement of the Registrar acting in his public capacity: "the Registrar, when exercising his discretion, is acting in a judicial capacity, not in an administrative capacity. Thus a decision to register is a judicial decision that the design is registrable, not that the Registrar approves of the design."

The concept of government speech is ostensibly implicated because national trademark offices are government agencies[333]/public bodies.[334] [335] Under the U.S. government speech doctrine,[336] when government speech is held to be operative, the contested speech - normally that of private (legal or natural) persons - escapes Constitutional (First Amendment) scrutiny. Thus, a 'government speech' designation is tantamount to a license to practice political bias ("viewpoint discrimination", according to the U.S. Court of Appeals for the Federal Circuit in The SLANTS, cf. "viewpoint

---

328 *Masterman's Design* [1991] RPC 89. This was an appeal to the Registered Designs Appeal Tribunal. Aldous J, "The Registrar, when exercising his discretion, is acting in a judicial capacity, not in an administrative capacity. Thus a decision to register is a judicial decision that the design is registrable, not that the Registrar approves of the design."

329 *Matal v TAM, 582 U.S. ____ (2017).*

330 *In re Old Glory Condom Corp.*, 26 U.S.P.Q. 2d (BNA) 1216, 1220 (T.T.A.B. 1993).

331 *Case: O-137-06, FCUK.* Trade mark Application Number: 2184549.

332 *Masterman's Design [1991] RPC 89.*

333 The United States Patent and Trademark Office (USPTO), established by the 1952 Patent Act (35 U.S.C. 1), falls under the U.S. Department of Commerce.

334 Public bodies are "formally established organisation[s] that [are] (at least in part) publically funded to deliver a public or government service, though not as a ministerial department." See 'Classification of Public Bodies: Guidance for Departments' issued by the Cabinet Office, available at: https://www.gov.uk/gover nment/uploads/system/uploads/attachment_data/file/519571/Classification-of-P ublic_Bodies-Guidance-for-Departments.pdf

335 The UK Intellectual Property Office (IPO) is an "executive agency" - a type of arm's-length (public) body sponsored by its home department (the Department of Business, Energy and Industrial Strategy) https://www.gov.uk/government/or ganisations/intellectual-property-office.

336 First articulated *in Rust v. Sullivan, 500 U.S. 173 (1991).*

neutrality").[337] In that case, the U.S. Court of Appeals for the Federal Circuit reminded the trademark office/government that it is not the keeper of speech.

In the GCC, the absence of precedents means there is no express position on this. However, the fact that third parties and organs of the state (the courts and the responsible Ministry)[338] can reverse the decision of the examiner is cited by practitioners in all three countries as evidence that a trademark examiner is not deemed a representative of the state and decisions are not state endorsement.[339] Furthermore, in the UAE, it is common for other government departments to refuse to recognise rights granted by trademark officials. For example, customs have stopped importation of products (not necessarily for public policy reasons) even when a trademark is known to be registered. Enforcement officials have also refused to enforce 3D marks or other non-traditional marks on the basis that they do not believe that the marks in question, registered in the UAE, are "trademarks".[340]

5. The government should not expend its time or financial resources to support marks that are contrary to the values of society

This rationale has been articulated by commentators such as Oswald[341] and in case-law such as *In re McGinley*,[342] and EU cases "Screw You"[343] (*Kenneth's Application*) and "fucking freezing".[344] In *In re McGinley*, the Court[345] expressly stated that Congress is not "legislating morality" when it prohibits registration under s2(a) of the Lanham Act, rather it is simply deny-

---

337  *In Re Tam* (n 74).

338  The responsible ministries are respectively the Ministry of Commerce and Investment in Saudi Arabia, Ministry of Economy and Commerce in Qatar, and UAE Ministry of Economy.

339  Article 21 of the UAE Trademark Law. Survey responses.

340  Survey responses.

341  Oswald (n 151).

342  *In re McGinley, 660 F.2d 481, 486 (C.C.P.C.1981)*. According to the case, Section 2(1) is a "judgement by the Congress that such marks not occupy the time, services, and use of funds of the federal government."

343  Second Board of Appeal, *Case R 1727/2014-2- 'fucking freezing! By TURPITZ (BILDMARKE)*;

344  Grand Board of Appeal, *Case R 495/2005-G – Kenneth's Application (Screw You)*.

345  United States Court of Customs and Patent Appeals (now Court of Appeals for the Federal Circuit)

ing the mark statutory benefits that it should not be afforded. It is possible that this is actually one and the same thing. This argument is also a government speech argument. The idea of the 'deserving trademark' was alluded to in "Screw You" and "fucking freezing!". Trademark registration was described as a "privilege".[346] Here, the Boards of Appeal seemed to argue that the morality and public order provision (Article 7(1)(f))) of the EUTMR is driven not by a censorial duty per se, but by an ethical one; to prevent the benefits of registration accruing to inappropriate trademarks.[347]

There is nothing to suggest that this notion of wasting state resources on undeserving trademarks features at all among examiners in the GCC.[348] This may be because these legal systems are relatively young and trademark officials are not yet inclined to question the role of trademark registers in society.[349] [350] It could also be because the GCC states *are* legislating morality.[351] This is supported by the prohibition on use of the disallowed sign.

## B. The problem of deceptively innocuous marks: trademarks accepted in error

In the GCC, there is a unique problem posed by English marks that are facially innocuous. There are two main ways in which morally objectionable marks that are facially innocuous, may be accepted. First, is **the specification in the application.**[352] The precise nature of the goods/service might be unclear to an examiner if the specification in the application form is written too generally. Certain Nice Classes clearly contravene the cultural and moral values of Gulf societies (e.g. Class 33) but many items fall into innocuous classes. Class 44 for 'medical services' is an accepted Class but a filing in Class 44 for abortion clinics/services would be rejected. In this case, the nature of the service is obvious from the application if "abortion" or a synonym thereof is mentioned. A less obvious service could in theory

---

346  *Kenneth's Application* (n 344) [13].

347  This ethical position ascribed to the EUIPO is by inference of this author.

348  None of the respondents selected this reason.

349  This is an inference made by this author based on postulation by Hansen (n 12) xxix, in relation to the nascent UAE legal system, that "perhaps because of these various facts, the professions appear not to participate in any kind of disinterested activism for reform of laws or procedures."

350  Normative propositions, in contrast, are prolific in U.S. and UK/EU legislative texts and jurisprudence.

351  Cf. *In Re McGinley*.

352  Survey responses.

be accepted in error. "*ASHLEY MADISON*" is an online matchmaking service to facilitate extra-marital affairs. It is registered for Classes 38 and 45, both of which are accepted in the GCC. Class 45 broadly covers "Personal and social services rendered by others to meet the needs of individuals." If the specification is worded too generally, in misleading terms,[353] or if it uses euphemisms, it could slip through. Perhaps the more foreign the concept is to Islam or to a conservative examiner, the less likely it is to cause objection. For example, an alien concept in Islam would be 'assisted suicide.' Suicide remains a strong taboo. "DIGNITAS To live with dignity to die with dignity" is a registered EU trademark in Classes 10, 16, 42, 43, 44, 45.[354] These are not prohibited Classes in the GCC. Medical services is a broad area. If an applicant filed in the GCC using the truncated form "DIGNITAS" in a bid to reach the large expatriate population through an online presence, and the specification was couched in terms like "dignity", "autonomy", "palliative care", it is conceivable that an examiner may not be alerted to the nature of the service.

The second way for immoral marks to pass without objection is due to **the particular examiner** who assesses the application.[355] It is not unusual for objectionable trademarks to be inadvertently accepted by GCC examiners who do not catch the meaning of the word mark. For example, the stylised mark *F\*\*K* was accepted in the UAE and published in the official gazette in early 2017,[356] despite evoking a vulgar connotation of the swear word "fuck". Even in the West, the threshold is high for this particular expletive.[357] The UKIPO and EUIPO have refused many phonetic and visual variations of "fuck"[358] because it is considered "deeply offensive" and would cause "justifiable outrage amongst a significant section of the pub-

---

353 In this example, 'marriage service', 'life is short' or 'social networking for married people or people in relationships'
354 International registration.
355 Survey responses.
356 Survey responses.
357 Notwithstanding some difficult-to-explain inconsistencies. For instance, EU-Registered trademarks include, JUST A FUCKING TSHIRT (006397103), FUCK LUCK (007024631). EU trademark protection was denied for the following, FIT FUCKERS (007497795), FICKEN, FUCK CANCER (012172722), FACK IT (014965701), NOYFB (015948359), FML Fuck My Life
358 FCK LDN was refused by the UK IP Office in May 2015 for Class 21 (UK00003109721). Available at: www.trademarks.ipo.gov.uk.

lic".[359] [360] The trademark FCUK was only accepted by the UKIPO because it was held not capable of being construed as the swear word "FUCK".[361] In a similar vein, *FCUK* has been accepted in five GCC countries.[362] Given the controversy surrounding the registration in the UK, this is noteworthy. One possible explanation is that the examiners in the region were not aware of the offensive connotation at the time of the registration. It could also be ascribed to the fact that the brand is famous (although fame must be judged at the date of application and some of these are not particularly recent). A third explanation for offensive marks such as this, appearing on the GCC registers is that evidence of parallel registrations in the GCC assuaged initial objections. There is precedent[363] from the CRIMINAL case that a rejection decision could be reversed on appeal by bringing to the official's attention a successful registration in another (more conservative) GCC state.[364] However, in another case this strategy failed.[365]

---

359  *Scranage's Application*, UKIPO Trade Mark Decision O-182-05, 24 June 2005, [11].

360  But see German Federal Patent Court decision overturning the rejection of "FICKEN".

361  In 2004, registered UK trademark "FCUK" was the subject of a third party cancellation action made in the public interest, based on Article 3(3)(a) of the Trade Marks Act. The action failed. The subsequent appeal, which was based on the same provision of law and a claim that the Registrar had erred in principle, was also dismissed. the decisions expounded principles that are instructive of the UK/EU approach to immoral trademarks.

362  Not Oman.

363  The term "precedent" is used here in a loose sense. There is no doctrine of precedent in the trademark registration system in question. Trademark offices are not bound by parallel registrations in other GCC states.

364  Successful registration in Saudi Arabia.

365  The trademark "KISSES" was rejected in Saudi Arabia and the rejection was upheld by the Administrative Court 6th circuit, 25 July 2017. The fact that there were many other "KISS" marks already registered at the Saudi Trademark Office did not persuade the officials to drop the objection. This approach is in line with the European approach: "the registrability of a sign as a Community trade mark must be assessed solely on the basis of the CTMR, as interpreted by the Community judicature, and not on the basis of previous Office practice" (judgment of 15/09/2005, C-37/03 P, 'BioID', [47] and judgment of 09/10/2002, T-36/01, 'Surface d'une plaque de verre' [35]

The earliest registration of FCUK is a Saudi Arabian registration date of 1999.[366] It was followed by Kuwaiti (2004, 2005),[367] U.A.E. (May 2005),[368] Bahraini (September 2005),[369] and Qatari registrations (2008).[370] But this explanation fails to explain how the most conservative jurisdiction allowed the FCUK mark in the first instance. The Qatari registration proceeded without rejection by the examiner and without opposition.[371]

Another surprising acceptance is ZIPPO. This is an example of a mark that is not offensive in English (indeed, would be considered fanciful) but has an offensive meaning in the local language, translating very closely to the male genitals. It is not acceptable to use in ordinary speech, either formal or informal. The trademark was accepted and registered in the UAE, Qatar and Saudi Arabia. This could be due to the fame of this brand for lighters. Interestingly, the trademark was rejected in Jordan.[372] Lastly, BUL-LOX is registered for tools (hammers) in Qatar and Saudi Arabia.[373] This could evoke the Middle English slang word of "bollocks", meaning testicles. It is used figuratively in colloquial English as an expletive meaning rubbish/bad, or useless/poor quality.[374] This problem of unknown words in English is also illustrated by the allowance of the trademark TIRAMISU for desserts.[375]

## Conclusion

This chapter teased out the motivations for prohibiting registration of immoral trademarks. It focused on the GCC with some rich insights from the US and Europe. It considered the role of public bodies and whether trademark registrability decisions are a mere judicial decision or a sanction. Dis-

---

366 Registration No. 141902217(502/53) - Class 25; Registration No. 141902218 (502/52) - Class 18.

367 Registration No. 57902 - Class 18; Registration No. 58153 - Class 25.

368 Registration No. 53301- Class 3; Registration No. 53300 - Class 18; Registration No. 53299 - Class 25.

369 Registration No. 45496 - Class 3; Registration No.45497 - Class18; Registration No. 45498 - Class 25.

370 Registration No. 33517 - Class 3; Registration No. 33518 - Class 18; Registration No. 33519 - Class 25.

371 Survey responses.

372 The mark was rejected in Jordan (survey responses).

373 Japanese company Imoto Hamano Co. Ltd for tools (hammers).

374 See: https://en.wikipedia.org/wiki/Bollocks.

375 Survey responses.

tinguished was the strict application of the law in the GCC and the more nuanced position in the West. It was determined that this was due to a few factors such as the civil law tradition in the Arab states, the young systems, the more stringent interpretation of moral norms, and the lack or subordination of free speech guarantees that tend to cultivate legal tests and guidelines for balancing interests.

It has been shown that in applying moral bars to trademark applications, the GCC and Western jurisdictions share common motivations. However, three main differences have been identified: 1) The concern that an offensive mark is undeserving of the state's resources and should be kept off the register is not thought to be a consideration in the GCC; 2) Shari'a principles are sometimes applied by the courts in conjunction with trademark laws, notably in Saudi Arabia. The principles expound the avoidance of harm and corruption; 3) There can be surprising decisions due to examiners being unaware of the meaning of an English (foreign) word or concept, or due to an unusually strict application of Shari'a by an examiner. The specification in the application may also sway the examiner towards the innocuous meaning.

The research for this paper indicates that all three jurisdictions are driven by a desire to prevent the public from feeling shocked or offended and that this is the primary rationale for refusing to register offensive trademarks. Shari'a principles have been recited in Saudi courts to prohibit registration of tobacco products. This is an example of Shari'a principles overruling both the trademark law and a social norm in the GCC (smoking) as Tobacco products are widely used.

# V. Moral thresholds – case law

*Introduction*

This chapter has two main components. Part A builds on the discussion of taxonomies in Chapter II and the idiosyncrasies of the GCC trademark system in Chapters III and IV, to present a harm-based taxonomy for immoral trademarks. Part B tabulates a small selection of GCC trademark decisions to expose thresholds [376] and provides brief insights where possible.[377] The chapter does not present a comprehensive review of GCC case decisions due to a lack of accessible data.

*A. Harm taxonomy*

This paper discussed current classifications of immoral trademarks in the literature.[378] Their limitations can be overcome by a two-layered taxonomy (Figure 4); it distinguishes the methodological task from the interpretatative task to avoid logic overlaps and construes the censurability of the trademark as the type of harm to which it contributes or causes.[379] This concept of 'harm' is employed as both a lens and a tool, to understand the social concerns that can be triggered by certain improper words/signs. It may also serve legal discussion of the sufficiency of a sign's impropriety to warrant state intervention. In this way, the taxonomy offers a 'language' grounded in harm, to improve alignment across jurisdictions in the treatment of this legislative area.

---

376 Thresholds operate at the second level (interpretative level) of the schematic.

377 Literature on trademark registration decisions is lacking in the GCC region, making it a very difficult-to-research jurisdiction. Nevertheless, this paper has attempted to draw out some idiosyncrasies in decision records.

378 See Chapter II(C)(III).

379 Contributory is used in relation to indirectly causing an act or series of acts (behaviour) by incitement (the direct harm is the resultant crime); causal is used in relation to directly evoking passive emotions (the harm is not physical).

Figure 4: New classification and taxonomy based on the concept of harm.

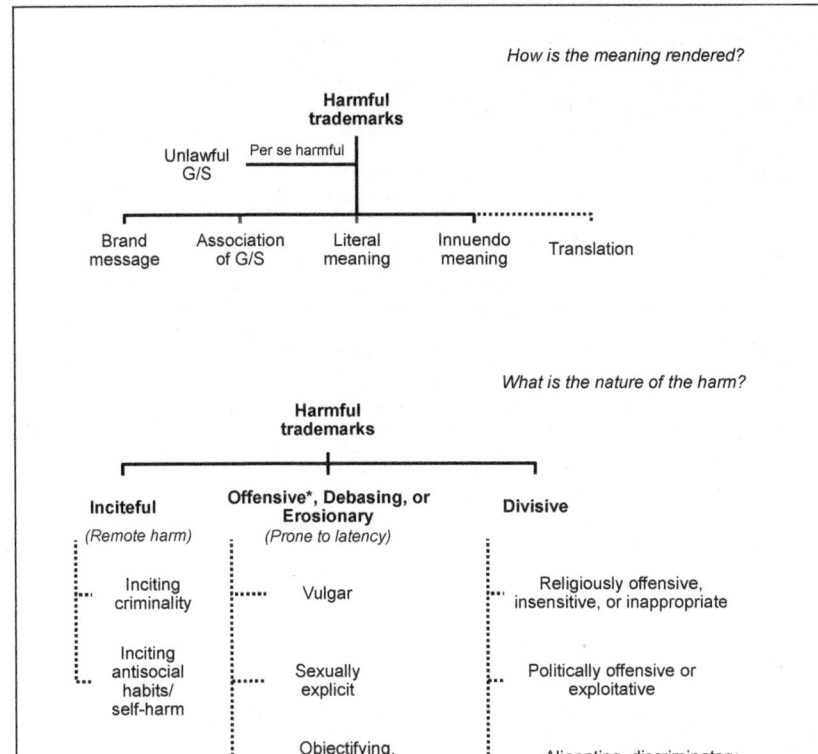

---

**INCITEFUL**
- **Inciting criminality**: e.g. violence, theft, rape, sedition. Contrary to law and order.
- **Inciting antisocial habits/self-harm**: e.g. suicide, anorexia. Harmful to public health or social integration.

---

**OFFENSIVE, DEBASING, OR EROSIONARY**
*Offensive means seriously morally offensive, suppresses human dignity, debasing, demoralising.
- **Vulgar**: harmful to societal values and personal dignity
- **Sexually explicit**: harmful to societal values and personal dignity
- **Objectifying, degrading, hypersexualising**: harmful to girls/women/those subject to hypersexualisation
- **Taboo**: harmful to inviolable/protected values.
- **Indoctrinational or totalitarian**: fanatical ideologies harmful to society and human dignity.

---

**DIVISIVE**
- **Religiously offensive, insensitive, or inappropriate**: harmful to religious sensitivities, tolerance and security
- **Politically offensive or exploitative**: harmful to political harmony and co-existence
- **Alienating, discriminatory, dehumanising/disparaging**: harmful to minority, marginalized, disempowered groups
- **Sectarian or tribal**: harmful to tribal identity and sovereignty, protection of religious sects.

---

*Nature of the harm*. Three categories of harm are proposed: [1] The first category is 'remote' or 'direct' harm and comprises "inciting trademarks" (trademarks **remotely connected [contributing] to the commission of a direct harm,** by incitement). Trademarks in this category threaten public safety, national security, and individual integrity and wellbeing, They are linked to behaviour. Thus, it is a public order category. With regard to tangible harm, there is a close connection. [2] The second category comprises "offensive, debasing or erosionary trademarks" that threaten to indirectly undermine moral values in society. Under this category, the desire to protect public morality is sufficient and no subsequent act/direct harm is necessary. However, this does not preclude the ability of such marks to perpetuate dangerous narratives and once ubiquitous, lead to direct harm. Latency, therefore, is a critical element in considering the harmfulness of such marks. Indeed, this harm may be more insidious. With regard to tangibility of harm, there is a loose, fragile connection. [3] The third category is a public order and social norm category. This category of trademarks is harmful to social cohesion and tolerance. These are "divisive trademarks". The harm relates to the ability to undermine societal values of tolerance and unity, with respect to religious, tribal, political, personal and other group affiliations and identity. Additionally, it is a morality category because the marks can be linked to offense against specific moral principles. UK courts have stated that the discrete moral principle that is offended against should be identified.[380]

## 1. Inciting trademarks

**Direct harm** is a public order category.[381] It links the trademark to a person's decision to commit a direct harm; that harm being a crime or engagement in antisocial/deleterious behaviour. Intervention is justified for the prevention of disorder and crime, and the safeguarding of public health and national security. There are two subcategories: (i) 'incitement to criminal activity' and (ii) 'incitement to antisocial habits'. When the imputation of the sign constitutes a criminal offence, it falls within the former subcategory. The latter subcategory covers suggesting or promoting harmful, deleterious activity that is not strictly unlawful. In some societies, a word may fall under a taboo, in other societies it may fall here. A trademark for a pro-anorexia website would fall under the scope of antisocial habits. A downstream extension of this logic is tobacco plain packaging legislation (censure based on the deleterious impact on health), smoking being neither illegal nor taboo. It is a truism that conduct may be both taboo and legally circumscribed.

## 2. Offensive, Debasing or Erosionary trademarks[382]

This category pertains to indirect harm and latency. Trademarks are harmful when, rather than inciting commission of a direct harm, they a) challenge human dignity, propriety or social identity and/or, b) perpetuate, cumulatively and over time, the erosion of society's moral values. According to this category, trademarks are censurable because they are seriously morally offensive such that they deliver an assault on personal dignity. But it goes further and proposes a 'risk' of more significant societal harm (and

---

380  *Basic Trademark* (n 9).
381  See discussion of public order in Chapter II, Part C.
382  Turner discusses levels of identity: core, social, group, role. Jonathan H. Turner, 'Revolt from the Middle. Emotional Stratification and Change in Post-Industrial Societies' (2017 Routledge).

potentially direct harm) when latently harmful trademarks accumulate and gradually exert an undermining effect on values. This follows "slippery slope" consequentialist logic.

*Indirect harm* is defined for the purposes of this taxonomy as: an instant affront to moral feelings, sense of propriety, or sense of security and dignity. It is evoked by gratuitously vulgar or sexually explicit signs.[383] This category is closest to and takes inspiration from U.S. trademark law's 'scandalous' matter. It differs by arguing for personal dignity as a right; more concretely, as a moral right to be free from insult.[384]

*Latent harm* is defined for the purposes of this taxonomy as proliferation and accumulation of signs over time, with the potential to lead to collective harm in the form of erosion of values, esteem, and connected behaviours or subcultures. This type of harm is potential, non-obvious and non-explicit;[385] it follows that applying a concept of latency incurs risks, notably that a) the harm (impact of the meaning) is not predictable at the time, b) once discovered, causation is difficult to establish and c) because it is by definition delayed, it becomes too late to correct.

There are five sub-categories:

(i) Vulgar
(ii) Sexually explicit[386]
(iii) Objectifying or degrading
(iv) Marks relating to a taboo: normalizing a taboo
(v) Indoctrinational or totalitarian (ideologies)

An example of a registered trademark that objectifies women is SLUT.[387] A trademark that is degrading would be, for example SLUTS STAY IN THE KITCHEN (fictional). Both are misogynistic and harmful to the social identity of women. US-registered trademarks SHANK THE B!T@H[388] and DIRTY WHOOOORE CLOTHING COMPANY[389] have no place on the

---

383 The adjective 'gratuitous' denotes that the context of the particular goods/ services cannot justify the word/does not negate its impact on the consumer as vulgar or explicit. This suggested addition would allow the sign "SCREW YOU" to be registered for sex toys, for example. In the GCC, this qualifying term would probably be redundant. See Hansen on parody (n 12).
384 Gan Shaoping and Zhang Lin, 'Human Dignity as a Right' (2009) Frontiers of Philosophy in China, Vol 4(3), 370-384.
385 Collins English dictionary (latent).
386 See (n 401).
387 SLUT (EU trademark registered 18/07/2005) – 003705084.
388 https://trademarks.justia.com/853/01/shank-the-b-t-85301216.html
389 https://trademarks.justia.com/857/23/dirty-whooore-clothing-85723806.html

register according to the standards of objectification of women and of social identity.

The violation of a taboo evokes a particular sense of alarm amongst society. It is difficult to determine whether a trademark represents a taboo as it is subjective and standards change. Extra-marital affairs, for example, may no longer be a taboo in the West. The trademark "ASHLEY MADISON" and "ASHLEY MADISON LIFE IS SHORT HAVE AN AFFAIR" is a registered UK trademark and the former is a registered EU trademark. Therefore, the UK Registrar, following the UK Trade Marks Manual guidance, perhaps does not consider it to be more than unsavoury conduct in modern day Britain.

A taboo mark could be one that risked normalising anorexia, such as the name of a "pro-anorexia" website. A mark that promoted suicide could also fall under taboo since suicide is not a criminal offence. Generally, when a mark crosses the line from taboo to criminal offence will not always be clear-cut. In the GCC, suicide is a sin (*haram*), not a crime as such and no criminal sanctions are set out in Shari'a law unlike other conduct. However, because it is a sin in Islam, attempted suicide has been punished criminally.

By proposing a harm-based approach, it is not argued that the survival of society is at stake. Rather, it is proposed that it is difficult to separate commercial speech from behaviour, and that trademarks at least have the power to influence perspectives. Accordingly, the thesis is that a proliferation of certain trademarks has the capacity to impact the collective marketplace in positive and negative ways and some can be significantly negative (perpetuation of inequities, objectification of women, for example).

## 3. Divisive trademarks

This is a public order category by virtue of the power of certain trademarks to alienate or vilify group identities and to exploit or perpetuate political, religious, tribal, and ethnic enmity. It includes signs that may symbolise organized oppression,[390] perpetuate victimization,[391] or threaten the sense of

---

390  For example, Case T-232/10 *Couture Tech ltd v OHIM*; Case T 232/10 *Coat of arms of the Soviet Union*, EU:T:2011:498

391  For instance, "Je Suis Charlie" (application 1668521, and "BIN LADEN" application (R-176/2004-2) have both been refused by the EUIPO.

safety or group identity.[392] This is in keeping with U.S. case-law, which has held that the application of the U.S. Lanham Act disparagement clause was most suited to religious groups.[393]

This category may be most similar to the disparagement clause in U.S. trademark law, but, driven by the harm concept, it emphasises the objective of the censure: to prevent symbols, imagery or messages that sow division, discord and alienation.

There are four sub-categories:

(i)   Religiously offensive, insensitive or inflammatory
(ii)  Politically offensive, exploitative, or victimizing
(iii) Alienating, discriminatory, dehumanising/disparaging
(iv)  Sectarian or tribal

### B. Case examples – marks refused on morality or public order grounds in the GCC

The following GCC trademark decisions explore consistency of harm thresholds in the GCC region. EU cases are compared.

INCITING
Incitement to criminality or antisocial habits

| Trademark | UAE | QATAR | SAUDI |
|-----------|-----|-------|-------|
| "CRIMINAL" | Initially rejected (registered following appeal) | Registered | Registered |

The undertaking Criminal Clothing Ltd. filed applications for "CRIMINAL" in the GCC countries. The application was rejected in the UAE for "violating the public morals or desecrating the public order." The UAE officials subsequently accepted the mark having been persuaded by registration certificates of other GCC countries including Saudi Arabia.

Similar marks rejected in the EU for suggesting or encouraging illegal activity are "HAIKIA", "STREAMSERVE", "ILC I LOVE COCAINE"

---

392  Turner (n 382).
393  As per the TTAB in In re Lebanese Arak Corp., 94 U.S.P.Q.2d (BNA) 1215, 1216 (T.T.A.B. 2010)).

"WORLDWIDE-STOLEN GOODS", "WEED", and "COPYCAT".[394] The fact that "CRIMINAL" was rejected in the UAE reveals a cultural difference. In the West, criminals may take on a mysterious, glamorous, misunderstood image (Bonnie & Clyde, the Kray twins, Hollywood films like Goodfellas). There have been registered trademarks for the music group "FUN LOVIN' CRIMINALS",[395] and for "BILLIE JEAN CRIMINAL".[396] This romanticism does not generally exist in the GCC. Interestingly, Europe bans from the register trademarks that glorify terrorism or offend its victims.[397] Here, it is possible that even a single victim would suffice to trigger the prohibition.

In "MECHANICAL APARTHEID", trademarks were said to have the ability to be "threatening".[398]

This category of marks, like marks with religious connotation, engage the idea of 'public order'. The jump from morality to public order appears to be "gross obscenity" which begins to impinge upon founding values of a society.

Islamic criminal jurisprudence recognises antisocial behaviour and the notion of that behaviour spreading throughout society: "Fasad fi al-ard" means "to corrupt the earth and destroy beauty of its creation" (Qur'ān, 2:27, 5:32). Terrorisms falls here and there have been many Islamic fatwas

---

394 HAIKA - 011610458; Judgement of 27 February 2002, STREAMSERVE, T-106/00; ILC I LOVE COCAINE – 013590948; WORLDWIFE-STOLEN GOODS – 013239827; WEED – 011953387; COPYCAT – 011870763.

395 001176361 (expired).

396 The mark is a reference to a Michael Jackson song. It is a cancelled EU trademark – 009297607.

397 The name of a terror group was banned in HAIKIA as contrary to public policy of the European Community. It was held that the fundamental values laid down in the CFR of the EU were precluded by absence of a right to life and to physical integrity. In this sense, terrorism strikes at these 'precursor rights'. The decision also suggests a presumption of public offence if such a trademark were registered; Offence to the victims was an express concern in MECHANICAL APARTHEID, see (n 310) [13], citing Case T 232/10, Coat of arms of the Soviet Union, EU:T:2011:498. "Signs that have no place on the register are certainly those which appear to glorify terrorism or offend the victims of terrorism (see 20.09.2011, T 232/10, Coat of arms of the Soviet Union, EU:T:2011:498)." In this cited case, the General Court upheld OHIM's refusal to register the trademark on public policy and accepted principles of morality grounds. The General Court deferred to the relevant public in Hungary, for whom the sickle, hammer and five-point red star symbolizes despotism.

398 MECHANICAL APARTHEID (n 310) [11].

against terrorist acts.[399] This is perhaps a 'collective marketplace' nuance but in respect of criminal conduct.[400]

OFFENSIVE, DEBASING, EROSIONARY
Sexually explicit[401]

| Trademark | UAE | QATAR | SAUDI |
|---|---|---|---|
| "RED HOT SEXY" | Rejected | Rejected | Rejected |
| "LA SENZA 24 SEXY" | Rejected | Rejected | Rejected |
| **Kisses** | Registered | Registered | **Rejected** |
| ![Kappa logo] **Kappa** | **Rejected** | Registered | Registered |
| ![figurative mark] | Initially rejected. Registered following appeal. | Registered | Registered |
| "ZIP" | **Registered** | Rejected | Rejected |
| "ZIPPO" | Registered | Registered | Registered |
| Various marks containing "KISS" "KISSES" | Registered | Registered | Registered |

In the case of "kisses", "ZIP" and "ZIPPO", it is the translated word that is offensive. This is in line with EU cases such as "FICKEN", FICKEN Liquors and "AIRCURVE".[402] However, in some cases the sensitivity of GCC officials is higher, as shown by the last two marks in particular. An immoral connotation was found in the back-to-back figures and the shape of the figurative mark presumably was suggestive of female reproductive organs.

---

399 See list of fatwas, rulings and authoritative statements against terrorism and related acts, according to the University of Melbourne's National Centre of Excellence for Islamic Studies, available at: http://arts.unimelb.edu.au/nceis/welcome/community-engagement/national-imams-consultative-forum/rulings-and-statements

400 Note that Islamic criminal law recognises offences against persons (*Qisas*, e.g. murder, theft, rape) or God (*hudud*).

401 Note, as per the tabulated examples, that 'sexually suggestive' is sufficient to meet GCC thresholds.

402 FICKEN – 009924275, 009274366; FICKEN Liquors – 010142123; AIRCURVE - Case R 203/2014-2.

While the above marks are at the subtler end of the spectrum, there is a question to be asked for brands that fall into this category. In relation to the type of harm that may flow from such marks, the question is whether the risk posed by sexually suggestive or profane marks is mere offence or a greater sense of personal invasion or assault - both of which are rather fuzzy and intangible-, or whether the accumulation of certain marks (that "transmit a message"[403]) begin to imprint on societal values and actually undermine them in tangible, measurable ways. This is beyond the scope of this paper but worthy of further analysis.

DIVISIVE
Religious issues[404]

| | Trademark | UAE | QATAR | SAUDI |
|---|---|---|---|---|
| 1 | "BUDDHA BEER" | Rejected | Rejected | Rejected |
| 2 | "CHURCH" | **Rejected** | Registered | Registered |
| 3 | | Rejected | Rejected | Rejected |
| 4 | | Rejected | Rejected | Rejected |
| 5 | dr.organic | **Registered** | Rejected (because of the Cross) | Rejected (because of the Cross) |

Marks 3-5 were rejected for being similar to the symbol of the Red Cross and the Red Crescent. This is consistent with international convention. However, the UK would have allowed these marks because they are not in red and white. White crosses on green background symbolise first aid goods and services; black and white depictions are also acceptable.[405] The

---

403 *Dick Lexic's Application* (n 9).

404 In the case of religious 'symbols', they fall under a separate provision not related to morality or public order. They are included here to demonstrate different thresholds.

405 Section 10.2 of the UK Trademarks Manual.

GCC rejections may indicate a reluctance to allow marks that resemble religious symbols in general. "CHURCH" for footwear was rejected in the UAE.

## Conclusion

This chapter introduced an alternative classification and taxonomy for trademarks falling under the morality and public order prohibition. It offered more granularity[406] and implicit recognition of subtle, progressive and cumulative infliction of harm. The classification framed and structured the public order and morality objection as a specific type or manifestation, of harm (divisive, erosionary, inciting). It acknowledges a problem of imputation (whether the conduct of autonomous individuals can be imputed to messages conveyed by symbols and signs). Further, because approaching the regulation of offensive trademarks from the perspective of remote or intangible harm has problems, a conceptual tool built in reliance is necessarily imperfect. 'Contingency' and 'causation' are not the only hurdles: a concept of harm that is not linked to tortious or criminal (physical) injury is prone to extension and arbitrary application; the idea of future harm is also insufficiently concrete.

With respect to jurisdictional differences, GCC decisions understood in light of Constitutional language, confirm a stronger inclination towards preventing harm. Despite GCC trademark law harmonisation efforts, there being different decisions particularly in the case of signs with sexual connotation means uncertainty for global brand owners.

---

406 For example, trademarks that objectify women are an additional sub-category, as well as trademarks that exploit tribalism or inflame sectarianism.

# Conclusion

This paper has sought to better understand the ways in which conservative cultures approach immoral signs. It did so by offering a new way of thinking about the impact of signs on society and the potential for tangible or latent harm. It began in Chapter I by presenting the challenges and tensions with limiting trademark protection and then set out the legal bases of such protection. It then dug into the landscape of GCC trademark law and proposed an appropriate approach based on the concept of harm. Some GCC trademark decisions were presented and considered in light of moral thresholds and regional harmonisation efforts. It is hoped that by adding more clarity to the position in the Gulf countries, more can be written about trademark practice in that Region and this will enrich the entire field. The insights presented in this paper were limited by a paucity of data. It would benefit from further research into the GCC in particular and multicultural settings in general.

# Appendix 1 – Survey of GCC law firms

*Dubai, United Arab Emirates*

Gowling WLG
  < https://gowlingwlg.com >
Cedar White Bradley
  < http://www.cwblegal.com >

*Doha, Qatar*

Abu-Ghazalah Intellectual Property (AGIP)
  < http://www.agip.com >

*Riyadh, Saudi Arabia*

Cedar White Bradley
  < http://www.cwblegal.com >
Saba-IP
  < https://www.sabaip.com >

# List of Works Cited

All sources are cited in accordance with the Oxford University Standard for the Citation of Legal Authorities (OSCOLA).

*Monographies and Articles*

Abdel-khalik J, 'Disparaging Trademarks: Who Matters' (2015) 20(2) Michigan Journal of Race and Law 288

Alemanno A and Bonadio E, 'Do you Mind my Smoking? Plain Packaging of Cigarettes under the TRIPS Agreement' (2011) J.Marshall Rev. Intell. Prop. L. 450, 462

Baird S, 'Moral Intervention in the Trademark Arena: Banning the Registration of Scandalous and Immoral Trademarks' (1993) 83(5) Trademark Reporter 661

Bonadio E, 'Brands, Morality and Public Policy: Some Reflections on the Ban on Registration of Controversial Trademarks' (2015) 19 Marquette Intellectual Property Law Review 43

— — 'Bans and Restrictions on the Use of Trade Marks and Consumers' Health' (2014) 4 Intellectual Property Quarterly 326

Bone RG,'Hunting Goodwill: A History of the Concept of Goodwill in Trademark Law' (2006) 86 Boston University Law Review 547

Brown Jr. RS, 'Advertising and the Public Interest: Legal Protection of Trade Symbols' (1948) 57 Yale Law Journal 1165

Carpenter M and Murphy K, 'Calling Bullshit on the Lanham Act: The 2 (a) Bar for Immoral, Scandalous, and Disparaging Marks'(2010) 49 U. Louisville L. Rev. 465

Cohen FS, 'Dialogue on Private Property' (1954), IX Rutgers Law Review 357

Dar HA and Presley JR, 'The Gulf Co-Operation Council: A Slow Path to Integration? ' (2001) 24(9) The World Economy 1161

Duff R and Marshall S, "Abstract Endangerment', Two Harm Principles, and Two Routes to Criminalisation' (2015) 3(2) Bergen Journal of Criminal Law and Criminal Justice

Ehteshami A, 'GCC Foreign policy: From the Iran-Iraq War to the Arab Awakening' in LSE Middle East Centre Collected Papers 1 (April 2015)

Fershtman C, Gneezy U, and Hoffman M, 'Taboos and Identity: Considering the Unthinkable' (2011) 3 American Economic Journal: Microeconomics 139

Fletcher A and Kera D, 'The forty-Fourth Year of Administration of the Trademark Act of 1946' (1991) 81 TMR 601

Gerhardt DM, 'Trademarks as Entrepreneurial Change Agents for Legal Reform' (2017) 95(5) North Carolina Law Review, 1519

Gibbons LJ, 'Semiotics of the Scandalous and the Immoral and the Disparaging: Section 2(A) Trademark Law after Lawrence v. Texas.' (2005) 9(2) Marquette Intellectual Property Law Review

Gilson Lalonde A & Gilson J, 'Trademarks laid bare: Marks that may be scandalous or immoral' (2011) Trademark Reporter 1476

Goble GW, 'Where and What a Trade-Mark Protects' (1927) 22 U. ILL. L. REV. 379, 388

Habachy S, 'Protection of Trademarks and Patent Rights in the Middle East History, Geography and Economics' (1962) 6 Patent, Trademark and Copyright Journal of Research and Education

Khoury AH, 'Ancient and Islamic Sources of Intellectual Property Protection in the Middle East: A Focus on Trademarks' (2003) 43(2) IDEA – The Journal of Law and Technology 151

Marks T and Betancourt JC, 'Rethinking public policy and alternative dispute resolution: negotiability, mediability and arbitrability' (2012) 78(1) Arbitration 19

McKenna MP, 'Testing Modern Trademark Law's Theory of Harm' (2009) 95 Iowa Law Review 63

Oswald L, 'Challenging the Registration of Scandalous and Disparaging Marks under the Lanham Act: Who has Standing to Sue?' (2004) 41 American Bus. L. J. 251

Palmer B, 'Saudi Arabia's Trademark Law' (1986) 1(3) Arab Law Quarterly 323

Pollack M, 'Your Image Is My Image: When Advertising Dedicates Trademarks to the Public Domain-with an example from the Trademark Counterfeiting Act of 1984' (1993) 14 Cardozo L. Rev. 1391

Ramsey LP, 'A Free Speech Right To Trademark Protection?' (2016) 106(1) Trademark Reporter 797

Scassa T, 'Antisocial Trademarks' (2013) 103(5) Trademark Reporter 1172

Schechter F, 'The Rational Basis of Trademark Protection' (1927) 40 Harvard Law Review 813

Shaoping G and Lin Z, 'Human Dignity as a Right' (2009) 4(3) Frontiers of Philosophy in China 370

Snow N, 'Free Speech & Disparaging Trademarks' (2016) 57 Boston College Law Review 1675

Spence M, 'The Mark as Expression/The Mark as Property' (2005) 58 Current Legal Problems 491

Stolte KM, 'How Early Did Anglo-American Trademark Law Begin? An Answer to Schechter's Conundrum' (1997) 8 Fordham Intellectual Property, Media and Entertainment Law Journal 505

Swann, Sr. JB, 'The Trademark Reporter as Catalyst' (2011) 101(1) Trade Mark Reporter 81

Wasserman DI, 'Trading Sex, Marking Bodies: Pornographic Trademarks and the Lanham Act' (2010) 23 National Black Law Journal

*Books*

Allan TRS, *Constitutional Justice: A Liberal Theory of the Rule of Law* (OUP 2001)

— — The Sovereignty of Law, Freedom, Constitution and Common Law (OUP 2013)

Ballantyne WM, *Essays and Addresses on Arab Laws* (Curzon Press 2000)

Batey M, *Brand Meaning* (Routledge 2008)

Bently L, 'The Making of Modern Trade Marks Law: The Construction of the Legal Concept of Trade Mark (1860-80)' in Bently L, Davis J, and Ginsburg C (eds), *Trade Marks and Brands.. An Interdisciplinary Critique* (CUP 2010)

— — 'From Communication to Thing: Historical Aspects of the Conceptualisation of Trade Marks as Property' in Dinwoodie GB and Janis MD (eds), *Trademark Law and Theory: A Handbook of Contemporary Research* (Cheltenham: Edward Elgar Publishing 2008)

— — and Davis J, and Ginsburg JC (eds), *Trade Marks and Brands. An Interdisciplinary Critique* (CUP 2010)

Bodenhausen GHC, *Guide to the Application of the Paris Convention for the Protection of Industrial Property* (as revised at Stockholm in 1967)

Davison MD, Horak I, and The Hon. Justice Gummow WMC, *Shanahan's Australian Law of Trade Marks and Passing Off* (5th edn, Thomson Reuters 2012)

de Carvalho NP, *The TRIPS Regime of Trademarks and Designs* (2nd edn, Kluwer Law International 2011)

Galligan DJ, *Discretionary powers: A Legal Study of Official Discretion* (Clarendon Press 1986)

Gibbons LJ, 'Trademarking the Immoral and the Scandalous: Section 2(a) of the Lanham Act' in Peter K. Yu (ed), *Intellectual Property and Information Wealth: Issues and Practices in the Digital Age* (Volume 3, Ch 4, Praeger Publishers 2007)

Hansen PW, *Intellectual Property Law and Practice of the United Arab Emirates* (OUP 2009)

Landolt PL, *Modernised EC Competition Law in International Arbitration* (Kluwer Law International 2008)

Lloyd D, *Public Policy: A Comparative Study in English and French Law* (London: Athlone Press, 1953)

Mill JS, *On Liberty* (J. W. Parker and Son 1859)

Phillips J, *Trade Mark Law; A Practical Anatomy* (OUP 2003)

Price D, *The Development of Intellectual Property Regimes in the Arabian Gulf States. Infidels at the Gates* (Routledge 2012)

Ramadan T, *Radical Reform: Islamic Ethics and Liberation* (OUP 2009)

Schechter FI, 'The Genesis of the Modern Law Relating to Trade-Marks' in Dinwoodie GB and Janis MD (eds), *Trade mark and Unfair Competition Law: Themes and Theories (Critical Concepts in Intellectual Property Series)* (Volume I, Edward Elgar Publishing 2014, and as reviewed by Hyland G, Columbia Legal Studies (2011))

Turner JH, *Revolt from the Middle. Emotional Stratification and Change in Post-Industrial Societies* (Routledge 2017)

*Other Secondary Sources*

CIA, World Factbook, www.cia.gov/library/publications/the-world-factbook/geos/sa.html

Edward Smith (2009), Absolute Grounds paper submitted by United Kingdom for SCT Assistant Principal Hearing, available at: www.wipo.int/export/sites/www/sct/en/comments/pdf/sct21/ref_uk.pdf

EUIPO, 'Guidelines for examination Trade mark, Part B Examination – Absolute Grounds of Refusal' (24 May 2016).

Gulf Labour Markets and Migration, available at: http://gulfmigration.eu/glmm-database/demographic-and-economic-module/?search=1&cmct=Saudi+Arabia

Johnson, 'Swearing: The Last Taboos' (Blog: Prospero, 21 January 2015), available at: https://www.economist.com/blogs/prospero/2015/01/johnson-swearing.

WTR Yearbook 2017 - Trade mark procedures and strategies: France (World Trade mark Review, available at: www.worldtrademarkreview.com/Intelligence/Yearbook/2017/Country-chapters/France)

WTR Yearbook 2017 - Trade mark procedures and strategies: Germany (World Trade mark Review, available at: www.worldtrademarkreview.com/Intelligence/Yearbook/2017/Country-chapters/Germany).

WTR Yearbook 2017 - Trade mark procedures and strategies: Italy (World Trade mark Review, available at: www.worldtrademarkreview.com/Intelligence/Yearbook/2017/Country-chapters/Italy)

*International Treaties*

Paris Convention for the Protection of Industrial Property of March 20, 1883; 21 UST 1583, 828 UNTS 305

Madrid Agreement Concerning the International Registration of Marks of April 14, 1891, as revised at Brussels on December 14, 1900, at Washington on June 2, 1911, at The Hague on November 6, 1925, at London on June 2, 1934, at Nice on June 15, 1957, and at Stockholm on July 14, 1967, and as amended on September 28, 1979

Protocol Relating to the Madrid Agreement Concerning the International Registration of Marks adopted at Madrid on June 27, 1989, as amended on October 3, 2006 and on November 12, 2007

European Convention for the Protection of Human Rights and Fundamental Freedoms, as amended by Protocols Nos. 11 and 14, 4 November 1950, ETS 5

TRIPS: Agreement on Trade-Related Aspects of Intellectual Property Rights, Apr. 15, 1994, Marrakesh Agreement Establishing the World Trade Organization, Annex 1C, 1869 U.N.T.S. 299, 33 I.L.M. 1197 (1994) [TRIPS Agreement]

WTO Agreement: Marrakesh Agreement Establishing the World Trade Organization, Apr. 15, 1994, 1867 U.N.T.S. 154, 33 I.L.M. 1144 (1994) [hereinafter Marrakesh Agreement or WTO Agreement]

European Patent Convention (1973)

*European Union Legislation*

Charter of Fundamental Rights of the European Union (CFR)

Convention for the Protection of Human Rights and Fundamental Freedoms (European Convention on Human Rights, as amended) (ECHR)

Regulation (EU) 2015/2424 of the European Parliament and of the Council of 16 December 2015 amending Council Regulation (EC) No 207/2009 on the Community trade mark [2015] OJ L 341

Council Regulation (EC) No 207/2009 of 26 February 2009 on the Community trade mark [2009] OJ L 78/1

Directive (EU) 2015/2436 of the European Parliament and of the Council of 16 December to approximate the laws of the Member States relating to trade marks [2015] OJ L 336

Directive 2008/95/EC of the European Parliament and of the Council of 22 October 2008 to approximate the laws of the Member States relating to trade marks [2008] OJ L 299

*UK Legislation*

Trade Marks Act 1994

*US Legislation*

Trademark Act 1946 (the 'Lanham Act')

*GCC Legislation*

Bahrain: Law No. (11) For the year 2006 on Trademarks

Kuwait: Decree-Law No. 68 of 1980 (Trademarks), as amended by Decree-Law No. 10 of 1987 and Law No. 1 of 2001

Oman: Industrial Property Rights Law (promulgated by the Royal Decree No. 67/2008)

Qatar: Law No. 9 of 2002 on Trademarks, Trade Names, Geographical Indications and Industrial Designs

Saudi Arabia: Law of Trademarks (promulgated by Royal Decree No. M/21 of 28 Jumada I 1423 (August 7, 2002))

Trademarks Law of the Gulf Cooperation Council States (2006)

United Arab Emirates: Federal Law No. 37 of 1992 on Trademarks (as amended by Law No. 19 of 2000 and Law No. 8 of 2002)

*Other national legislation*

Brazil: the Law on Industrial Property (9,279/1996)

Chile: Industrial Property Law (19.039)

Egypt: Law No. 82 of 2002 Pertaining to the Protection of Intellectual Property Rights

France: Law 1991-7 of January 4, 1991 on Trademarks and Service Marks

Iran: Patents, Industrial Designs and Trademarks Registration Act of the Islamic Republic of Iran (2008)

Iraq: Law No. 21 of 1957 on Trademarks and Trade Names

Jordan: Law No. 33 of 1952 on Trademarks amended by Law No. 34 of 1999 Amending the Trademarks Law

Lebanon: Laws and Systems of the Commercial and Industrial Property in Lebanon Resolution No. 2385, issued on January 17th, 1924, amended by the Law of 31 January 1946

Libya: Article 5(b), Trademarks Law

Malaysia: the Trademarks Act 1976

Morocco: Law No. 17-97 on the Protection of Industrial Property (as modified and supplemented by law 31.05)

Poland: Act of June 30, 2000, on Industrial Property (consolidated version of November 29, 2013)

The Republic of Sudan: The Trademarks Act (1969 Act No.8)

Turkey: Decree-Law No.556 Pertaining to the Protection of Trademarks in force as June 27, 1995

*Cases*

*EU*

C-487/07 L'Oreal SA v. Bellure NV [2009] ECR I-05185

R 0495/2005-G – SCREW YOU; R 495/2005-G – SCREW YOU

R 111/2002-4, Dick Lexic Limited's Application (Dick and Fanny)

R711/199-3, Myles Ltd's Application, 5 December 2001 (OHIM)

T-232/10 Couture Tech ltd v OHIM

Je Suis Charlie Trademark Application 1668521

*UK*

Fook Trade Mark Application O-182-05

Ghazilian's TM Application [2002] R.P.C. 628

Philips Electronics NV v Remington Consumer Products Ltd [1998] ETMR 124

French Connection Ltd., No. 2184549 v. Woodman, No. 81862, Dec. O-137-06 (May 17, 2006) (U.K.)

Masterman's Design [1991] RPC 89

Basic Trademark SA's Trade Mark Application O-021-05 [2005] RPC 25 (Jesus Trade Mark decision)

Arsenal Football Club plc v. Mathew Reed [2001] ETMR 860

*US*

In re Old Glory Condom Corp., 26 U.S.P.Q. 2d (BNA) 1216, 1220 (T.T.A.B. 1993)

In re McGinley, 660 F.2d 481, 486 (C.C.P.C.1981)

Matal v. Tam, 582 U.S. ___ (2017)

In Re Tam, 808 F.3d 1321 (Fed. Cir. 2015)

Pro-Football, Inc. v. Harjo, 415 F.3d 44 (D.C. Cir. 2005)

In re Lebanese Arak Corp., 94 USPQ2d 1215 (TTAB 2010))

Mishawaka Rubber & Woolen Mfg. Co. v. S.S. Kresge Co 316 U.S. 203, 205 (1942)